Go
Your
Own
Way

Go Your Own Way

A Practical Guide for Women Walking the Camino

ANDREA WAIT

Published 2024
Printed in the United States of America
Print: 979-8-9894049-3-3
E-book: 979-8-9894049-4-0
Library of Congress Control Number: 2024907670

Cover and interior design by Tabitha Lahr
Cover photos © Shutterstock.com

Contents

*To all the Lady Pilgrims of the world —
thank you for showing me the Way.*

Foreword →

Dear Reader,
What an adventure you are about to undertake; I am so excited for you! I've walked the Camino twice, and the second time I was lucky enough to walk it with Andrea. Wherever your starting point is, Andrea will help you prepare for the journey you're inspired to take. We each have our own style of travel and walk, and as you set out on this journey, you'll need to discover (if you don't already know) what yours is.

Take, for example, the different styles Andrea and I have when it comes to the Camino: Andrea has clarity and attention to detail. I, on the other hand, tend to rely on things naturally working out.

What I realize now, of course, is that I could have this carefree approach on my second pilgrimage because I was with Andrea. She had made reservations for our lodging for each day, so I could focus on the walk and my own thoughts. After an especially grueling day, it was Andrea who found out where to get a massage or booked a hotel that had a pool. Her generosity and careful planning were what made my adventure so fluid.

I wouldn't say it was *easy*, but it was worry-free. She observes what everyone needs and thinks carefully about details most of us don't realize are important until after the fact.

In these pages, she will help sort out any nagging questions that may seed doubts in you as you embark on walking the Camino. This book will help give you perspective and offer guidance without ever attempting to control your journey.

Andrea's generosity comes naturally to her. Take, for instance, her method of packing. My style is throwing things in a suitcase—not much planning as far as what I needed, and thus taking a number of items that never see the light of day during the journey itself. Andrea, on the other hand, had a small bag armed with key items suited for any and all situations. When it rained, she had a windbreaker and rain poncho; when there was a pool, she had a swimsuit; when her feet needed a much-deserved rest, she had comfy sandals.

She thought every detail through, even down to our daily packs. When I'd decide to stop after a few hours of walking to rest and get my café con leche and a small snack, I'd be flustered, struggling to get my wallet out of my backpack. Andrea, in contrast, always had a fanny pack so her wallet was at the ready. It's those small details that made the adventure easier. (Needless to say, I've bought a fanny pack since then.)

The year Andrea and I walked the Camino, the heat was brutal, so Andrea would set out early in the morning. I, on the other hand, had a different routine; I liked to ease into the day, so I was usually a few hours behind her on the path. I dedicated each day of my walk to someone I knew—a friend or a family member—and as

I walked, I'd think of the person I'd chosen that day and what they meant to me. I often wished that I had some token to leave behind in memory of that dedication.

As I was walking along, I would stop to refill my water bottle or rest and every now and again I would see small stones with words or names that I recognized. They'd been left by Andrea. Again I would be in awe. Not only had my friend packed well, she had even made space for the small tokens she wanted to leave along the way.

I am hopeful that this book will allow you to set out on your walk feeling what Andrea's presence felt like to me: a friend's hug. It perhaps won't fully answer all of your questions or resolve all of your doubts regarding this huge endeavor; however, it will offer you the helping hand you need to start your journey.

Ultreia!

—Gladys Dalmau

CHAPTER 1

Buen Camino →

Considering a journey on the Camino de Santiago? Perhaps you've been inspired by the film *The Way* or perused one of the many guidebooks out there, and it's sparked your interest. However, some hesitation holds you back from making the commitment. If you're like me—a woman of a certain age enticed by the notion of solo trekking 500 miles (or, in European measurement, 800 kilometers)—an inner voice is probably raising concerns like, "Are you crazy? You've never walked such a distance," or "Do you really think you can manage this alone? Are you nuts?"

I hope this book silences that critical voice and emboldens you to declare, "I am going to walk the Camino."

We all possess the potential for a more resonant, encouraging inner voice. I want to help you tap into it. I've always cherished Oprah's quote about the Universe sending us messages—first a whisper, then a louder voice, and finally a resounding yell.

Well, consider this book to be your resounding voice, proclaiming, "YOU MUST GO WALK THE CAMINO!"

I apologize for yelling—but the Camino is absolutely worth a good old-fashioned shout.

I too harbored several reservations about this adventure—until I faced a cancer diagnosis two years ago. Those ominous three words—*You have cancer*—shifted my perspective. I had walked parts of the Camino before and, each time, had entertained the thought of walking the entire French Way route "one day." But every time I considered it, my inner naysayers would chime in:

You don't have the time.
You're not physically up for it.
It's too costly.

And, the most nonsensical of all:

What will people think?

My diagnosis rendered my excuses irrelevant. While my surname may be Wait, cancer conveyed the message that there was no time for anything of the sort.

After listening to that message and ultimately completing all 500 miles of the French Way, another message urged me to share my journey, with hopes of inspiring other women to embark on this amazing, life-transforming experience.

There are already numerous Camino guidebooks out there, as I mentioned earlier. But whereas all those other books are primarily focused on where to go and what to see, mine aspires to transform your aspiration from "I want to walk the Camino" to "I *am going to* walk the Camino." I want to address all those perceived obstacles holding you back in the most encouraging, loving, and supportive way—and smash them to bits.

What qualifies me to do this? Having worked as a professional organizer for the last fifteen years, I've honed the art of organization at home *and* during travel adventures. These skills proved invaluable on my Camino journey. This guide breaks down my experience—what worked and, importantly, what didn't—and provides suggestions for overcoming the various fears and issues you're likely to encounter before and during your own walk.

I won't sugarcoat it—walking the Camino isn't easy. But it's far and away the most rewarding endeavor I've ever undertaken and I think it can be that for you too.

CHAPTER 2

Fear →

The first obstacle you may face when considering walking the Camino is plain old fear, which comes in all shapes and sizes.

Many of my female friends have expressed a desire to walk the Camino but often qualify it with statements like, "I would love to walk the Camino, but I am fearful of [fill in the blank]." Recently, for example, a woman named Eileen shared with me that the biggest challenge wasn't even related to the walk itself: "I'm scared about how I will get to the start of the walk," she told me. Her fear was centered around *transportation*—a seemingly manageable concern!

Our conversation unfolded as follows:

Me: Where do you live?

Eileen: Chicago.

Me: All right, one option is to fly to Madrid, take a train to Pamplona, and then either catch the 11:00 a.m. bus to Saint-Jean or share a cab to SJPP with other Pilgrims waiting outside the station, easily identifiable by their giant backpacks and walking poles.

Eileen: Oh! That actually sounds pretty easy.

This interaction prompted me to reflect on whether other women's fears might be similarly straightforward. Could their obstacles, like Eileen's, be easily addressed?

One of the things I love best about women is how freely we share and discuss fears and solutions with one another. With this in mind, I did some crowd-sourcing as I wrote this book. As a result, in the pages to come, you will not only get my thoughts and advice but also hear from other lady Pilgrims offering valuable suggestions for how to make the Camino what I like to call "doable."

As the Roman philosopher Lucius Annaeus Seneca said, "A man who suffers before it is necessary suffers more than is necessary." Well, the same goes for women—and while I can't take your worries away, I can at least offer you some solutions to drastically minimize your suffering!

Let's not let imagined problems hold us back. We are much stronger than our perceived fears.

PHYSICAL FEARS

It's not safe.
Safety was paramount for me as a solo female walker. While I've been lucky to avoid any dangerous situations, the experience of residing in two metropolitan cities, New York and San Francisco, has taught me the importance of taking precautions. These are some steps I suggest for you:

1. Limit walking to daylight hours.
2. Stay vigilant, paying constant attention to your surroundings.
3. Use only one earbud while listening to podcasts and music to remain aware of ambient sounds.
4. Keep your personal belongings close, especially in more urban settings with large numbers of people.
5. Utilize a fanny pack to secure essential items, minimizing the risk of leaving them behind.
6. Regularly check the Facebook Camigas page for updates from fellow Pilgrims.
7. Monitor the weather daily.
8. Be cautious about disclosing solo walking to strangers; instead, share stories of Camino friends met along the way.
9. Don't walk out the door in fear, with eyes cast down. Walk out onto the road with eyes wide open and see it all.
10. Listen to your gut. If something feels strange, respond accordingly. That can be as minor as crossing the street to avoid someone who makes you feel uncomfortable.

While I've never felt fearful while walking, I have always taken care to be mindful at all times. And over time I've tapped into a supportive community of female Pilgrims who, through a combination of verbal check-ins and WhatsApp messages, helped me feel protected and cheered on.

I can't walk and carry my backpack.

Issues with carrying my backpack emerged during my initial Camino journey from Leon to Santiago in 2018, during which I covered distances of ten to twenty miles a day. To say I was naïve about how difficult this would be is an understatement—I simply thought, *I'm just walking. What's the big deal with carrying my stuff?*

Then came the "never-ending day," a pivotal moment when I realized if I truly wanted to reach Santiago, a change to my approach was imperative. It took me *thirteen hours* to get to my destination that day, and I definitely had moments where I thought, *I should just lie down on the side of this path and accept that this is the end of me.* Yep, I was tired (and, shall we say, a tad bit overdramatic, considering the fact that there is always a Pilgrim walking ahead of you and one walking behind you, so you're never really alone on the Camino), and I needed to make a change.

As I trudged along, I reflected on the advice an Irish lady in a pub earlier that day had offered upon seeing my bright red, exhausted face: "Be Jesus, deary," she exclaimed, "get a courier!"

I encountered similar suggestions from a variety of locals, including a pharmacist who tended to my feet and the albergue owner who saw me stagger through the door at 8:00 p.m. at the end of that thirteen-hour day.

Okay, I thought, *I need to alter my approach.*

The very next day, I hired a luggage transport service. If I was to be successful in this journey, I needed help, and there was no shame in that.

This was an important lesson for me—and it's one that I think so many of us women need to embrace. You know how flight attendants always advise us to put on our own oxygen masks first before helping others? Well, as the saying goes, a man needs to be told that only once—but a woman has to hear it twice. Sure, it's a generalization, but in my experience, it's nearly always true. Women are raised to put the needs of others before their own, and as a result, many of us balk at asking for help. That was certainly the case for me.

Do you want to know the even deeper truth? Part of me didn't want to hire the luggage service because I felt as if doing so would be "cheating", and I worried what people back home would think of me if I didn't carry my own pack for the entire route.

Writing this, I can see how ridiculous that sounds. I was choosing to walk 500 miles by myself, and yet I thought I would be a failure if I didn't carry my pack. So silly. That was my second lesson: what other people think of me, both at home and on the trail, is unimportant.

Now, if you're inclined to carry your pack, go ahead and give it a try. I did . . . and then I didn't. Just know that whatever you decide is right for you, *it's okay*, and so is changing your mind. If you initially decide to carry your pack and then find halfway through your journey that doing so has become overwhelming, remember you can always reconsider and enlist the help of a luggage transfer service.

Entering the Camino with numerous self-imposed rules, I swiftly learned the importance of adapting to what worked for me. The Camino offers diverse ways to navigate, from the distances covered each day to the accommodations available to the mode of transportation—hiking, biking, horseback riding, or using bus and taxi services is all possible. The key is to figure out what works best for *you*—a valuable insight that is, incidentally, also applicable to our everyday lives.

You will learn when you head out there are many Camino sayings. One of the best ones I learned was, "The only way is Your Way."

I don't know if my feet and knees can handle it.
There is an abundance of information available on optimal care for feet and knees on the Camino. Personally, after a few days of hiking and dealing with blisters, as well as experiencing pain in my knees, hips, and back, I realized that even without a pack to carry, my current approach was just not working. I needed a more comprehensive routine for caring for my entire body.

My solution? **RSMFK.**

Rest: Recognizing the importance of sleep for mental, physical, and emotional recovery, I chose not to succumb to the pressure of early-morning starts. While my fellow Pilgrims hurried to begin their day, I prioritized sleeping until my body naturally signaled it was ready to wake up. I always booked my accommodations in advance, ensuring a stress-free end to each day (unlike some of my fellow Pilgrims, who winged it each day and faced the risk of hearing "No room at the inn" upon arrival). I also booked single rooms, another luxury—no roommate translated to no disturbances, like snoring. This allowed me to wake up refreshed and ready to tackle the trail each day. I was always amazed by how a good night's sleep could take me from feeling achy and sore to refreshed and ready to start the day.

Stretch: I designed a fifteen-minute stretching routine for my hips, knees, ankles, and spine. It became a daily practice for me, helping me mentally prepare for the day ahead and wind down for a good night's sleep. Stretching proved to be a valuable ally to me on the Camino, swiftly alleviating occasional cramping episodes. It was not only good preventive medicine, it also provided incredible relief when I woke up in the middle of the night with a pain in this, that, or the other body part. My Camino expression: "When in doubt, stretch it out."

Meditate: To dispel early-morning anxieties about the day's hike, I adopted a simple twenty-minute meditation practice. This ritual replaced unwarranted worries with a sense of peace and joy, setting a positive tone for the upcoming journey. If you don't have a practice yourself, there are great apps out there that can help. (I like Insight Timer!) I found that at the end of each session, I felt calm and excited about heading out for the day rather than nervous about what was to come.

Foot care: I religiously applied Vaseline to my feet and socks both morning and night, ensuring a blister-free experience throughout my journey. Your feet are what will get you from the start to the finish, so you must take care of them. I also routinely switched out my inserts, toggling between the pair that came with my shoes and a pair of Superfeet women's orthotic shoe inserts. Just having that small change made my feet feel better and reenergized.

Knee care: Be mindful of the toll long-distance walking takes on knees (especially if you're a fifty-eight-year-old with knee surgery in your past). I found relief in stretchy knee sleeves that provided compression. Putting them on daily right after lunch became a ritual that rejuvenated me, reinforcing the belief that my body could conquer the day's challenges.

I also am a huge proponent of what's called a TENS machine, which regularly came to my rescue any time I was experiencing persistent pain. TENS devices offer relief through pulsations applied to targeted spots on the body (in my case, the joints). In moments of widespread fatigue and soreness, my TENS machine, which resembles a TV remote with wires attached to sticky pads, proved indispensable. While the initial sensation may be peculiar, perseverance led to gratitude as the pain subsided. I sometimes even used it in the middle of the night when I needed relief.

This device can be purchased online or at your local pharmacy and is relatively inexpensive, but remember to make sure you have the batteries needed to operate it before you set out on the Camino.

Walking the Camino inevitably involves physical challenges, but it also teaches the vital lesson of self-care. Simple practices like adequate rest, stretching, meditation, and targeted care for feet and knees all remind us as we journey of the broader importance of self-care in our day-to-day lives.

I know, I know . . . another Camino lesson!

I don't know if I have the right shoes.
The key to successful walking lies in your choice of footwear! While countless blogs offer recommendations on the best Camino shoes, the crucial factor is finding the pair that make your feet feel the best. I often playfully mention my "blessing" of having wide clown feet. In my past Camino walks, hiking boots and heavy sneakers all resulted in aching feet and multiple blisters by day's end. This time, preparing for the total 500-mile walk, I invested time and money in discovering the perfect pair for me. Fortunately, I stumbled upon the Altra brand, which is renowned for its wide toe box. The second I tried them on, it was evident that these shoes were tailor-made for my feet. This time, there were no blisters.

I can't stress this enough—invest the effort in finding the right shoe for you! Outdoor retailers like REI boast knowledgeable salespeople who not only understand feet but also how to factor in elements like distance and terrain. Many of these experts are familiar with the Camino and can provide personalized recommendations for your journey.

In addition to your hiking shoes, bring some kind of sturdy, open-toe sandal. (Trust me, your feet will be thankful for the occasional switch-up.) Personally, I like Birkenstock's EVA sandals. They are lightweight and sturdy, and my feet were happy whenever I put them on. Plus, if you happen to stay in a place where the shower is . . . not so clean . . . these shoes can get wet, which translates to no fungus on your feet!

Blisters will ruin the experience for me.
Even when you take all possible precautions on the Camino, blisters can happen. It's crucial to be prepared

with essential supplies to address them when they do. Here are the steps I've followed for treating blisters on the Camino. (Disclaimer: Not everyone may agree with this approach; this is simply what I've personally found effective in healing my feet and allowing me to continue walking despite those ugly bubbles!)

First and foremost, try to be proactive and address your feet at the first sign of a "hot spot"—typically, a sensation of heat, tenderness, and mild pain. If you find yourself experiencing any of these warning signs, follow these steps:

- Stop walking.
- Sit down.
- Remove your shoes and socks.
- Examine the area for signs of discoloration and blistering.
- If the foot is simply red, massage the area and stretch out your foot for blood circulation.
- If you have some time, consider lying on your back and putting your legs up against a wall (or tree, or post, or whatever stable thing you can find) to drain some fluid from your feet, ankles, and legs.
- Apply Vaseline and a fresh pair of socks. I was always amazed how great my feet felt after just changing my socks.

If a blister has already formed, take immediate action with your blister kit, which you should be carrying with you daily. That kit should include a safety pin, antiseptic cleanser, skin cleaner, and blister bandages.

Again, not everybody agrees with this approach—

but speaking from my own experience, this is what worked for me every time:

- Clean your hands and the blister.
- Sanitize the safety pin with rubbing alcohol.
- Using the safety pin, make a small hole at the blister's edge.
- Gently squeeze out *all* the fluid. Ensuring complete drainage is crucial; otherwise, the blister may refill.
- Clean the area again and gently pat dry.
- Apply antibiotic ointment and let it dry for a moment.
- Cover with blister plaster.
- Leave it alone until the bandage falls off.
- Toe blisters. If you find yourself with a blister on your toe, making it uncomfortable to walk, consider using Dr. Frederick's toe protectors, which are available in various sizes. By applying these protectors, your toes will be kept apart to minimize friction and allow you to walk with ease and comfort.

If you follow these steps and still experience pain while walking, it's possible that you haven't completely drained the fluid from the blister or may have developed an infection. In such a situation, do not power through the pain; seek medical attention. I recall a Pilgrim friend who ignored his own foot discomfort only to find himself in the hospital a few days later, undergoing toenail removal—which, of course, abruptly halted his Camino journey.

Something I hope you find reassuring: Foot injuries are common on the Camino, which means that if medical intervention *is* necessary, you'll receive top-notch foot care. Healthcare professionals in this region are well versed in treating "Camino feet"!

I won't physically be able to do it.
After having maintained a daily average of walking 10 miles at home for a few months before heading out on this journey, I confidently assumed I could handle my ambitious plan of covering an average of 17 miles a day on the Camino. Sometimes I just have to laugh at my naïveté.

Reality hit me hard once I was there; by the fifth day of walking, doubts were creeping in about whether I'd ever reach Santiago. Feeling overwhelmed, I sought support from Camigas, the Facebook women's group, asking for virtual support. The encouraging words I received in response proved invaluable. The most helpful advice came from one woman who emphasized a seven-day adjustment period for physical, mental, and emotional strength. Her advice addressed the challenges I faced: physical exhaustion, self-doubt, sadness, and anxiety. Following her counsel, by the eighth day, I found my stride.

If you're apprehensive about the physical demands of the Camino, take heart in the fact that options abound — including shorter distances, planned rest days, and alternative modes of transportation. During my own journey, I witnessed fellow Pilgrims who, unable to walk the entire way, opted for buses or cabs to get them to the finish line.

If walking remains your ultimate goal, training before your trip, with varying elevations and terrains, is a good idea. But whatever your goal, it's crucial not to fixate on perfection. Try to embrace the idea that there can be myriad paths to your destination; having choices can alleviate mental stress. Who knows—just knowing you have choices could give you greater fortitude, and you may surprise yourself with the distance you can cover.

Remember: You must do what works best for you on the Camino. If that means skipping a segment of the walk that's too difficult for you, that's more than okay.

What if it's cold and rainy?

My foremost concerns while planning my Camino journey surrounded the potential discomfort of being cold and wet. Luckily, while rain and dropping temperatures are inevitable, there are effective measures you can take to combat them.

To ward off the chill, I packed a lightweight beanie, a highly insulating hoodie, and slim, stretchy yoga pants. These pants not only served as daily attire but also functioned as makeshift long underwear beneath my hiking pants on particularly damp and cold days.

Addressing the challenge of rain, I equipped myself with a rain poncho, rain pants, a backpack cover, and waterproof shoe covers. Given that damp feet can lead to blisters, the shoe covers proved indispensable.

When it comes to this aspect of the Camino, do as the Scouts do: be prepared. With the right gear, you'll be able to handle any storms that come your way.

What if it's too hot?

Alternatively, there's the flip side: the Camino can get quite hot during certain times of year. With that in mind, when plotting out your Camino journey, consider what season you will embark. Of course, with how much our climate is changing, unforeseen heatwaves (and cold snaps!) may occur, and even the most meticulous planning can't always save you. If you're heat-sensitive, here are some measures you can take to improve your experience:

1. Opt for early-morning walks.
2. Wear a quality sun hat.
3. Choose clothing made from materials that wick away sweat.
4. Carry a lightweight scarf to shield your skin from the midday sun, preventing sunburn and keeping you cooler.
5. Drink lots and lots of water. Hydration—a.k.a. your water bottle—is your friend.
6. When reserving accommodations, try for places with air-conditioned rooms—and a pool. A refreshing swim can work wonders as a healer after a day of walking. Plus, just knowing you have that cool water waiting for you at the end of the day can makes that day's walk go by fast—really fast.

I'm still not sure I have the right clothes!
Test all your clothing items before departing. Confirm that each piece fits well, feels comfortable, and fulfills its intended purpose. (For example, does your raincoat effectively keep you dry during a downpour?)

My big lesson on clothing was when my pants split right down the front seam during a practice walk in the rain. Seems that COVID weight gain had changed my figure, and I needed a bigger pair of pants! Thankfully, I was still at home and had time to order a replacement.

Getting hurt and being unable to finish.
These two concerns come together into a two-pronged apprehension—physical injury and the prospect of not completing the journey.

Let's first delve into the realm of injury. Accidents can happen anywhere, and occasionally, we find ourselves hurt. I encountered a woman who experienced a fall resulting in a broken shoulder while on the Camino, forcing an untimely end to her journey. However, there was a silver lining: the support of fellow Pilgrims who rallied to assist her, ensuring she received excellent medical care. The underlying message here is not to let life's "what-ifs" hinder your progress. As that Pilgrim later told me, "I met the nicest people who really cared for me, which I haven't experienced in a very long time. And I am planning to continue my walk next year, right where I left off."

So, yes, falling is a very valid concern. Walking sticks can be your best friend on the Camino. I opted for lightweight carbon fiber poles with cork handles. The pair I carried could be easily broken down into three individual poles and stored not only in my day pack but also in my carry-on bag, which meant no unnecessary hassles while going through airport security.

The second worry here—not being able to finish the adventure you've started—is understandable, but if that's the only thing standing between you and the Camino, it's time to rethink things. Yes, the thought of not reaching the endpoint is a disheartening one—but that's all it is, a *thought*. You won't know what you're capable of until you're there. Is the fear that you might not measure up really sufficient rationale to forgo embarking on this incredible journey?

This is a question only you can answer and I hope your answer is *no*.

A difficult recovery post–Camino, also known as pain and cramping.

First and foremost, consult with your physician to determine whether undertaking the Camino walk is advisable for you. If they say it's safe for you to go, ask about preventive measures against cramping. Are there any supplements you could take that will help your body during and after the walk, or any specific stretches you should incorporate into your routine? Seek your doctor's guidance on effective strategies for preventing muscle issues like cramping and stiffness.

Secondly, if you know your body tends toward cramping, swelling, or stiffness, plan for shorter daily distances to avoid reaching the point of strenuous exertion. Incorporate rest days into your schedule at regular intervals as well, so your body periodically has a chance to recover. Originally I had no rest days planned on my Camino trip—and as you will learn, my "forced" rest day turned out to be one of my favorite of all my thirty-eight days walking!

MENTAL/EMOTIONAL FEARS

I'm worried that I won't be able to stay connected to my family while I'm gone.

No need to fret. In today's era of advanced technology, numerous cost-effective methods allow you to stay connected. Consider installing apps on your phone, such as Spot Tracker, Strava, and WhatsApp. For Apple devices, you can also use Find My Friends. Enhance your family's tracking capabilities by attaching an Apple AirTag to your bag, allowing them to follow along with you from afar every step of the way. Establish a Facebook page to keep friends and family informed about your daily adventures. Additionally, consult your phone carrier to assess international costs, as some providers offer unlimited data plans.

I am directionally challenged.

Before discovering the Camino, I had considered hiking the Pacific Coast Trail. However, being aware of my limited map skills, the extent to which navigating the PCT requires map-reading scared me off. As a relatively inexperienced hiker, I wanted to channel my focus and energy into the journey itself, rather than constantly worrying about getting lost. So I sought a route that would naturally guide me without relying on maps—and that's where the Camino came in!

One aspect I truly appreciate about the Camino is the clear trail markings, such as clam shells and yellow arrows on the ground, along with other easy-to-spot structures early on. Later, there are mile markers. These visual cues ensured that I never lost my way. While it's still possible to deviate a little bit from the path, especially when you're fatigued at the end of the day, modern technology is always there to get you back on track. With your trusty smartphone, navigating back on track will be a breeze if you ever do find yourself off course; it's rare to find yourself without cell phone service. And in case all else fails, a simple gaze behind you might reveal another Pilgrim, allowing for the old-school approach of just asking for directions!

I don't speak Spanish.
One of my regrets is that, during my training, I didn't dedicate any time to learning Spanish. Nevertheless, as an English speaker, I recognize my fortunate position. People come from all over the world to walk the Camino, and English often serves as the universal language. While there were some instances when my conversational partner spoke only Spanish, we always managed to communicate through hand gestures and facial expressions—or by utilizing Google Translate, which is also a useful tool to have on your smart device. However, it would be to your benefit to learn some basic phrases—"Where is?" (*¿Dónde está?*) and "How much is it?" (*¿Cuánto es?*) are two good ones to know—before embarking on your journey. It will help you get what you need, yes, but perhaps more importantly, Spanish is the language spoken in Spain! You are a visitor to someone else's home when you're on the Camino, and even knowing simple expressions like "good morning" (*buen día*) and "hello" (*hola*) will get you a lot more enthusiasm and kindness from your hosts.

I'm worried about not "fitting in" with other Pilgrims.
No matter your age, the concern of fitting in is a shared human experience. However, the reality is that the

Camino will naturally connect you with like-minded individuals. I embarked on my journey solo—planning to walk and dine alone. Yet fellow Pilgrims often extended invitations, transforming solitary moments into shared experiences. What started with casual greetings at rest stops evolved into heartfelt exchanges of "nice to see you" and then, eventually, "how's it going?" Without consciously seeking it, I began recognizing Pilgrims by name, and by the second week, which coincided with my birthday, I had formed a small circle of friends.

My Camino friend group added immeasurable joy to my journey. They surprised me with a birthday cake and a cheerful happy birthday song on my big day, they offered encouragement along the trail, and they kept connected with me through WhatsApp messages. Before long, I had made two new best friends, both named Maria, who infused my Pilgrimage with laughter and lasting memories. (We eventually became known as Maria, Maria, and Not Maria.)

In essence, fitting in isn't a prerequisite; the Camino unfailingly provides connections. All you need to do is trust in the journey, and it *will* deliver. And here I go with another famous Camino expression—one you will hear many, many times, possibly even in this book:

The Camino provides.

I'm afraid of the unknown.
The unfamiliar can evoke fear, yet it also holds the potential for wonder. Here are a couple of things to bear in mind if you're feeling nervous about what you don't know.

First, recognize your own resourcefulness in navigating challenges. Life brings unexpected twists, and your response to them defines the outcome. I discovered this about myself at the conclusion of one taxing day on the Camino. Exhausted and hungry, I arrived at my designated albergue for the night, only to realize I had botched the reservation. There were two establishments with the same name in the region—and I'd booked the one located 60 miles away. I can't completely explain in words the feeling I experienced when I realized this, but the closest I can get is to say that I felt *doomed*. I was hungry and tired, and visions of having to sleep outside were swimming through my head. Essentially my brain took me from *Hurray, you made it to your destination!* to *You're homeless for tonight.*

Faced with this dilemma, I could have succumbed to the emotional distress, but I forced myself not to panic and instead coached myself into a calmer state. *I'm all right*, I reminded myself. *I just need assistance sorting this out.* I did a physical scan of my body; surprisingly, I was in pretty good shape. Then I noticed that in my line of sight was a kitchen, meaning I could get food there, and across the room was a bathroom, meaning I didn't have to panic about—well, you know.

Then came the best realization of all: the front desk clerk spoke English and Spanish, meaning she could help me figure this problem out. I explained the situation and asked for her aid, and in no time we'd figured out a solution. I decided to proceed to my next destination ahead of schedule, which surprisingly wasn't too far away. Since I was ahead of my planned itinerary, I opted to stay there for two nights and enjoy a well-deserved rest day. Although I initially had to spend the night in a communal dorm room (which turned out to be a valuable experience), the following night, the compassionate front desk clerk upgraded me to a delightful suite with a bathtub. On that restful day, the rain provided the perfect backdrop for me to indulge in a soothing hot bath and several refreshing naps in the most comfortable bed I've ever encountered. What initially seemed like a misstep turned out to be a blessing I'll always cherish. It provided the rejuvenation my body, mind, and soul truly needed!

Moral of the story: Situations arise, but it is our responses to them that can determine the outcome. The Camino is undeniably a remarkable setting where both Pilgrims and those offering services are eager to assist one another; indeed, this mutual support is among my favorite aspects of the experience.

Yes, you need to plan for your trip, but it's also crucial to remain open to the twists and turns it could take. Fear is a natural emotion, but as with anything, it's our approach to it that can make a difference. Think of the Camino as a beautifully wrapped birthday present, concealing the unknown—a gift brimming with the potential for a once-in-a-lifetime adventure.

I need my morning coffee.
My morning coffee ritual holds immense importance for me, and at home I relish the leisurely pace at which I savor my first cup of the day. Prior to beginning the Camino, I stressed about whether I would have to rise, dress, and head out the door every morning before consuming my essential cup of morning brew. Recognizing the need for a strategy, I devised a plan. Upon reaching my destination each day, I would scout out the coffee situation for the following morning—would the albergue provide it, or would I need to venture out? Fortunately, this wasn't usually an issue, and I delighted in the places

where unlimited coffee and hot milk were dispensed from sizable silver pots. Enjoying my favorite morning beverage alongside my fellow Pilgrims first thing in the morning set a splendid tone for the day ahead.

I have dietary restrictions—I'm anxious about the food situation.

One of the most demanding aspects of my Camino journey proved to be the culinary experience. Initially, I enjoyed the bread, meat, and cheese dishes I kept encountering, but as time passed, my body began to crave vegetables.

Another challenge was the late dinner service—typically after 7:00 p.m., which was less than ideal after a long day of walking. I preferred dining at 5:30 p.m. To adapt, I had to proactively plan by locating grocery stores (to ensure a supply of fruits and vegetables) and restaurants with earlier serving times along the way. Thankfully, there are many Camino apps that will help you plan ahead to find what works for you. If your dietary restrictions are a big concern for you, you might even consider bringing some supplies from home that will meet your needs.

LOGISTICAL CONCERNS

Booking rooms.

Having completed sections of the Camino three times previously, I was determined to prearrange my accommodations when I did the full walk. Understanding that hiking 500 miles would already present a significant challenge, the prospect of searching for lodging at the end of an exhausting day seemed too daunting.

While some may argue that prebooking goes against the spirit of the Camino, it proved to be the most practical approach for me. Ultimately, the choice of how much planning you want to do for this aspect of the trip is yours to make. Fortunately, the convenience of apps and websites like Booking.com has streamlined the reservation process, making it easy for you to plan and book in months, days, or even mere hours in advance.

During my recent Camino journey, the increasing number of walkers posed a significant challenge for many Pilgrims who had *not* booked in advance. If you find yourself in such a situation, start by calmly approaching other Pilgrims with a simple inquiry: "Where are you staying?" Engaging in conversations may reveal available options for the night that you weren't aware of. Additionally, if you've reached out to a place and they claim to be full, don't hesitate to ask if they can guide you to an alternative. I've personally found the individuals working at the albergues to be exceptionally kind and supportive.

Enlisting the help of a local can significantly improve your chances of finding lodging compared to attempting it on your own. You may think you are in this all by yourself, but again, the Camino is a collective of people who are happy to help one another. At some point, you may need to get out of your comfort zone and simply say, "I need help."

Going to the bathroom outside.
This can pose a significant concern for women, and the reality is, it's essential to become comfortable with the idea of using the outdoors if you're going to walk the Camino. I suggest you practice during your training hikes prior to departure. Embark on a hike, find a secluded spot behind a tree, and handle the situation. It's as straightforward as that. And in the unlikely event that someone catches a glimpse of your exposed backside, don't let it bother you. Everyone does it (on the Camino, anyway)!

One more thing: Please, whatever you do, don't hold back on drinking water during the day to hold off having to pee. Dehydration can lead to all sorts of health issues. So drink water—lots of it—and when nature calls, answer it.

Getting the time off work.
Yes, there is Wi-Fi in most places, so if you have to work, you can. But ideally, this experience of a lifetime will be a chance for you to be present in your journey and step away from work. If there's any way you can make that happen, do it!

Not sleeping well.
Lack of sleep is a valid worry. If you stay in shared rooms, most likely there will be noise, a.k.a. snoring. So this is where you ask yourself, *How important is it for me to have a quiet room?*

Being particularly sensitive to noise, I opted for a private room every night and utilized wax earplugs to ensure a more peaceful sleep environment. It worked like a dream.

Bed bugs.
First, let me be clear: I didn't have an issue with bed bugs on my walk! But if you do encounter any during yours, there are effective ways to address the issue. According to online sources, heat, such as from hair dryers, and rubbing alcohol can be effective for eliminating them (or at least staving them off). In my case, I carried a small spray bottle containing a homemade mixture of lavender hand sanitizer and rubbing alcohol, and upon reaching my room each day I diligently sprayed the mattress, sheets, and pillows. Lavender is supposed to be a deterrent against bed bugs, and it also added a pleasant aroma to my bedding. As for the heat option—I definitely wasn't going to carry a hair dryer as I walked, but many places did have them in the bathrooms.

Congratulations on reaching the end of my list of concerns! You may have additional worries that I didn't address here, but here's the crucial point: setting off on the Camino is a true embodiment of "experience of a lifetime." Don't let your fears hinder you. As a friend recently advised me, "Yes, you may be scared, but don't let that hold you back—instead just go ahead and do it, even if you have to do it scared."

CHAPTER 3:

Preparation →

Individuals vary in their approaches to preparation. This is what I did. Perhaps it will work for you—or at least give you some ideas as you formulate your own plans.

FITNESS

The most straightforward way to prepare yourself is to start walking anywhere and everywhere you can. I set a goal of covering 10 miles a day leading up to my Camino journey, and for the most part, I achieved it. The only adjustment I would make now, looking back, is to incorporate longer walks with my day pack full of supplies, and to include varying elevations and terrains in my training.

All that said, let's be realistic: regardless of how much you train, the Camino will present challenges, and that's an integral part of the experience. Give training your best effort, walk as much as possible, but ultimately, the true test will come when you're actually on the Camino.

I recall, on a day a couple of weeks into my walk, looking at my planned mileage for the next day and thinking, *Tomorrow I have to walk only 12 miles!* With time and experience, your perspective changes; what once seemed formidable becomes shockingly manageable. Truly, it is a day-by-day thing.

HANDS AND FEET

Ensure that your nails (hands and feet) are trimmed short and all calluses, particularly around the heels of your feet, are removed before you embark on your trip. I recommend doing this about a week before your departure; you don't want your skin to be too tender when you start your journey, and that week of buffer will give your feet a chance to toughen up a bit posttreatment!

YOUR STUFF

Like I said before—try out everything you buy, from your shoes to your clothes to your first aid kit items! What works for one person may not work for you, so be *personally* familiar with everything you're bringing along before you go. If you've decided you're going to carry your own pack as you walk, get yourself fitted at a local mountain store, such as REI, to make sure you're packing your items with proper weight distribution and that the backpack itself fits you properly.

PILGRIM PASSPORT

To obtain the Compostela certificate upon completing your Pilgrimage, you have to obtain a Pilgrim passport and collect stamps daily as you walk. You can get the passport in advance by preordering the credential at www.americanpilgrims.org (also an overall good source for Pilgrim information) up to three months before your start date.

MONEY STUFF

ATM card: Check that your security code is four digits, as many places adhere to this limit. If your code is longer, consider changing it.

Cash: Contrary to common belief, it's unnecessary to obtain euros before arriving in Europe. Instead, you can simply withdraw cash from an ATM upon arrival. ATMs are also readily available along the way, and many of the Camino apps will point you to exactly where each one is located.

Credit card: Before your journey, verify whether you need to notify your bank/credit card company of your travel plans—and if you do, do it!

CELL PHONE

Find out ahead of time what your plan's international fees are. To circumvent any unpleasant charges, consider installing the WhatsApp app on your phone for texting and calling loved ones back home (it works on Wi-Fi, so you don't have to use up cellular data). It's also an excellent means of connecting with fellow Pilgrims worldwide, as it allows communication with international numbers at no additional cost. (This is how most of the world outside of the United States communicates, FYI!)

MAIL

If you're someone who gets a lot of snail mail at home, it's probably worthwhile to place a temporary hold on your deliveries. I set mine to delay deliveries until a couple of days after my return so I wouldn't be overwhelmed with mail on my first day back—and I really feel it allowed for a smoother transition back to "real" life.

CHAPTER 4

What to Bring ➔

Whether you decide to carry your belongings or opt for a luggage transfer service, managing the amount of items you need to bring with you on the Camino requires constant mindfulness. In navigating "the stuff," three crucial elements come into play: the container (luggage), the contents (your clothes, toiletries, and gear), and the organization (packing cubes).

Remember, I'm a professional organizer—when it comes to packing, I don't mess around! Here's how I approached it.

LUGGAGE AND ORGANIZING CONTAINERS

It might seem a bit obsessive, but I consistently packed my bag in the exact same order each and every day. I adhered to this routine without deviation, and the result was remarkable—I never had to rearrange my belongings, and not a single item went missing over the course of my thirty-eight days on the Camino. Maintaining this consistency allowed me to quickly identify any gaps in my suitcase, eliminating the risk of leaving something behind. (It's worth noting here that losing items is so common among Pilgrims that there's even a Camino Lost and Found Facebook group page!)

At the end of the day, when fatigue sets in, preserving the limited energy left in your tank is crucial; whatever juice you have should be directed toward eating and self-care, not trying to figure out where your belongings are.

What I used
- Kipling Darcey small carry-on rolling luggage
- Travelon packing cubes (small, medium, and large)
- GoToBag organizer storage packing bags (three-pack)
- Bagsmart clear toiletry kit with zipper
- Pack All water-resistant zipper pouch

How I packed my suitcase
Large cube—weather
- Raincoat/poncho
- Rain pants
- Waterproof shoe covers
- Cotton beanie
- Zipper hoodie
- Bandana
- Cotton scarf

Medium cube—daily clothes
- Tank top
- Short-sleeve T-shirt
- Long-sleeve T-shirt
- Stretchy hiking pants
- Shorts
- Baseball hat

Small cube—undergarments
- 6-pack of underwear
- Sports bra
- 10-pack of white crew socks
- Pajama pants (stylish enough to look like pants when doing laundry)
- Travel laundry bag

Bagsmart clear toiletry kit—toiletries
- Mack's earplugs in bright orange (easier to find in my bag)
- Soap
- SPF face lotion
- Toothbrush
- Toothpaste
- Hair ties
- Hairbrush
- 2 travel-size hair conditioners
- Small travel-size deodorant
- Vaseline
- RiptGear knee compression brace
- Wipes (for face, body, and dusty shoes)

Bagsmart clear toiletry kit with zipper—first aid kit

- Aleve
- Dr. Frederick's Original Better Blister Bandages
- Dr. Frederick's Original Soft Gel Toe Protectors (great for blisters between toes)
- Safety pin
- Active Skin Repair spray
- Nuun Sport electrolyte tablets (to add to water)

Pack All water-resistant zipper pouch— electronics

- INIU portable charger
- Easy@Home TENS unit
- Sunbeam GoHeat USB heating pad
- 6-in-1 USB universal charging cable
- Mobile phone charger
- iPad
- iWatch
- iPhone

Free-floaters

- Altra Lone Peak sneakers
- Superfeet women's orthotic shoe inserts
- TheFitLife carbon fiber trekking poles
- 2 small plastic containers for food
- Water bottle

DAYPACK

On the Camino, what kind of day pack you use and how you pack it are equally important. I used a Cotopaxi Batac 24L backpack, because I liked how lightweight it was. I did, however, add a waistbelt to it for stability and proper weight distribution.

How I packed my daypack
Outside sleeve
- RiptGear knee compression sleeve (I tried out many, and these are the best; they don't slide and you can move them higher up or lower down the leg depending on the location of your pain)
- Extra pair of socks (change out midday, every day)
- Scarf wrap (great for sun protection and temperature control)

Inside main compartment
- Small toilet paper roll and plastic bag
- Food containers (full of food left over from breakfast or bought at a market)
- Fruit
- Daily small first aid kit—Vaseline, sun block, Aleve
- Crocs (if there is flat terrain for the day, these can be a nice alternative to your sneakers)
- Walking sticks
- Mobile phone charger

FANNY PACK

I chose a fanny pack with three compartments. The innermost back compartment is for valuables you want to ensure remain secure against your body and less susceptible to theft. The interior and front pockets are convenient for items you want quick and easy access to.

How I packed my fanny pack

Back compartment

- Passport
- Large bills

Interior compartment

- Phone
- Earbuds
- SPF lip balm
- Gum/mints
- Tissues

Front compartment

- Small bills for purchases while you're on the go

HOW TO PACK WHEN YOU'RE CARRYING EVERYTHING . . . MEANING NO LUGGAGE TRANSPORT SERVICE!

Again, selecting the right backpack is crucial to your comfort. Drawing from my own experiences, I've learned a few things on this subject:

- Start by laying out all the items you intend to take with you and categorizing them on your bed.
- Assess the volume needed to accommodate your belongings and determine the appropriate backpack size.
- Conduct some research to identify the backpack that suits you best. I recommend checking out the Camigas Facebook page, where women who know what they're talking about can address your specific questions.
- Pack your items into your chosen backpack and bring it to an outdoor retail store so they can assess everything. (Personally, I favor REI; they're not only great at ensuring your pack is a proper fit for you, they're also happy to provide valuable advice on optimal packing techniques.)
- Once you start your walking training, assess what you need and what you can let go of. You will be amazed by how many things you will quickly feel willing to say goodbye to. As the saying goes, "less is more."
- Last but not least—remember, just because you planned to carry your backpack every day

doesn't mean you have to keep doing it no matter what! If it ever becomes overwhelming, know you have the option to take a break and utilize a luggage transfer service.

CHAPTER 5

Tips Galore →

find joy in receiving helpful tips from others—hopefully you do too! In this chapter, you'll discover my own recommendations, along with several shared by fellow Pilgrims, for various aspects of preparing for and walking the Camino. Some of it I've covered to a limited extent in previous chapters—but for those topics, I'm adding something new here, I promise!

BOOKING ACCOMMODATIONS IN ADVANCE

When organizing your journey, consider breaking it down into manageable segments over time. For example, when arranging accommodations for my trip, which required planning for thirty-nine lodgings, I opted to book five places each day, which typically took me about an hour. Within eight days, I had secured all my accommodations—without breaking a sweat. This method proved so effective that I ended up applying it to all aspects of my planning, from obtaining supplies and making travel arrangements to creating playlists and downloading podcasts. Within less than a month, I'd taken care of every detail—and because I was doing it bit by bit, I never felt overwhelmed.

TRAINING

Similar to planning your trip, consider breaking up your training over an extended period of time. If you have a year until your walk, use that time wisely. If you're not already a big walker, begin with shorter jaunts—perhaps just half an hour at a time—and gradually increase their duration over the course of the year. As you build endurance, add in different types of terrain and increase your elevation gains. Every step of the way, listen to your body—acknowledging what feels comfortable versus what seems like excessive exertion. Your optimal training zone lies between these two points, and this awareness can guide you in planning the distances you aim to cover each day on the Camino.

It's worth noting that most Pilgrims typically walk an average of four to twelve hours per day, consistently, throughout their journey. That is a big range of time, so be sure to find *your* sweet spot.

SUPPLIES

I know I've said this already, but I can't emphasize it enough: before embarking on your trip, test *everything* out in advance. Some other things to consider:

- When you're walking as much as you do on the Camino, your feet swell. Consider getting shoes that are one size larger than you might normally buy for added comfort.
- Safety pins are incredibly versatile, so attach at least one to your backpack—you may be very glad later that you did.
- Pack only the essentials—bring exactly what you need, and leave unnecessary items at home. If you find somewhere during your journey that you really need something you didn't bring along, there are plenty of stores along the Camino where you can buy additional supplies.

BATHROOM BREAKS

When I asked my good friend Gladys what her best piece of advice on walking the Camino was, she told me this: "Never pass up using a bathroom. If you see one, use it, as you don't know when you will see one again." I couldn't agree more!

FOOD

When placing an order at a bar or café, consider paying immediately to avoid unnecessary waiting. Trust me, this can become quite frustrating over time. Planning ahead by researching what is available along your route, including options for food and bathrooms, will also save you lots of time and effort. Keep in mind that supermarkets are often closed on Sundays, so plan any weekend restocking you need to do for Saturday.

HYDRATION

I cannot overemphasize this: water is your friend! Drink lots of it. I added a hydration tablet twice a day to my water bottle. Not only did it give me a much-needed electrolyte boost, it also offered variety—it was nice to mix things up with a flavored drink here and there.

LAUNDRY

Make a note of the laundry services available at your booked accommodations. While most places provide laundry supplies, not all do, so consider bringing laundry sheets with you just in case—they work great, and they take up less space and weigh far less than liquid detergent.

During check-in at your accommodation, ask about the location of the laundry room. If it's on the ground floor, take the dirty laundry out of your bag right away at check-in to bring directly there instead of going to your room first. Sometimes the host will take it for you;

sometimes you have to take it directly to the machine. Either way, doing this right away saves you from carrying heavy bags up and down stairs more than you need to (remember, you're going to be very, very tired!), and it might also mean you getting a head start on laundry before other Pilgrims arrive.

PACE

"Unlike your regular life, take your time; it is not a race." I love this quote from one of my fellow Pilgrims. We humans all come in different shapes and sizes; my five-foot-five stride is different—very different—from a six-foot-tall man's stride, for example. I found when I tried to keep up with certain people, I got even more tired than I needed to, because not only was I moving faster than my body wanted to, my brain kept telling me, *You can't keep up with this person*—which stressed me out. I promise you, it is absolutely okay to say, "Hey, I am going to slow down here for a bit," and let whomever you're walking with go ahead without you. If you feel you've made a connection and want to see them again, ask for their number and make a plan to meet up later in the day.

PACKING LIST

Make a list of your top essentials *first*—things like your passport, phone, and any medications you know you need to bring with you. After that, you can add the extras. That way, if your pack ends up being too heavy, you'll know where to look to knock off some of the weight (i.e., the bottom of your list!).

PHARMACY

If you come across an open pharmacy and realize you're running low on an essential supply, stop and stock up immediately. Don't wait until the next day, as pharmacies may not always be readily accessible. I learned this lesson the hard way when I discovered I am allergic to dogwood trees. I kept arriving in villages during siesta, when their pharmacies were closed, so I was stuck without allergy meds. I didn't have clear breathing for three days—not a great situation when walking the Camino.

TIME TO WALK AND TIME TO STOP

Start your daily journey in the early morning. As one fellow Pilgrim so eloquently put it, "Walking in the morning equals two hours of walking in the afternoon." So get out early and walk, and when your brain starts to wonder, *Where's the next town?*—stop and take a break, even if only for five minutes. Even a brief pause can make such a difference in body and in mind.

RECOVERY

At the end of the day, adopt the practice of elevating your legs against the wall to alleviate inflammation. Another Pilgrim also recommends, "After your day's walk and shower, put on knee-high compression socks." When possible, treat yourself to a soothing foot and leg massage (or just do it yourself!), and as I emphasized earlier, stretch every night. And when needed, don't hesitate to take anti-inflammatory medication to enhance your daily recovery process.

Last but not least, plan periodically for a full day off, commonly referred to as a "rest day" on the Camino. Your body will thank you for it.

SAFETY

Although I found the Camino to be incredibly safe, there are times where you may check into a place—in a larger city, for instance—and realize the people staying in the same lodging as you are not Pilgrims, so it's time to be a little more mindful. One thing I like to do in this situation is to request two room keys, as this gives the impression that I'm not traveling solo. I have even gone as far to speak to an imaginary person inside my room after opening the door, giving off the impression that I am not alone. Safety first!

SANTIAGO

Register for an appointment to obtain the Camino "Compostela"—the accreditation for the pilgrimage—in Santiago to avoid feeling rushed on your final walking day. I suggest registering the morning after you arrive in town so that on your arrival day you can just focus on celebrating your incredible accomplishment: finishing the Camino!

Allocate a couple of days to stay in Santiago. This city is the culmination of your journey, so take the time to savor the achievement and allow your body to recuperate after your long and arduous trek. And if you want to enhance your experience there, I highly recommend signing up for the rooftop tour of the cathedral, which you can purchase tickets for in advance online.

MORNING ROUTINES

I had a ritual that I performed faithfully every morning, and it helped me get my head right before starting my day's walk. I'll share it with you here, in the hopes that getting a more concrete idea of what a morning on the Camino is like will be helpful to you:

- Use wipes to clean shoes. (I like having clean shoes when I start the day.)
- Check the weather to decide what layers to bring.
- Dress accordingly.
- Pack belongings, ensure that the courier tag on your luggage accurately indicates the destination for the day, and place it in the building lobby by 8:00 a.m. for the courier.
- Fill up your water bottle and add Nuun hydration tablets.
- Eat breakfast.
- Stretch. Stretch. Stretch.
- Meditate.
- Apply Vaseline to your feet.
- Apply sunscreen to exposed skin.
- Put on your hat.
- Conduct a *thorough* check of your bathroom and bedroom, including sheets and blankets,

to ensure nothing has been left behind. Having to backtrack to retrieve something you've forgotten is simply awful.

- Use the toilet, even if you don't think you need to.
- Put on your fanny pack and day pack.
- Grab your hiking poles.
- Start walking—with a smile!

CHAPTER 6

Encouraging Words ➝

As mentioned earlier, on my fifth day of walking, I grappled with the decision of whether I could continue all the way to Santiago. My body, mind, and soul were exhausted. I was ready to call it quits. I considered reaching out to the friends back home whom I would usually turn to in crisis, but in this case I realized they might not fully comprehend the challenges I was facing. So, I instead sought support from the women's Facebook group I've mentioned a few times now, Camigas. Their encouragement played a pivotal role in helping me reach my destination.

Here's what I wrote that day:

Hello Camigas. I just got to Pamplona, and it was a long, hard day. I'm worried I won't make it to Santiago and could use encouragement. I appreciate any help you can provide. Love, Andrea

Here are some of the uplifting responses I received:

Andrea, my walk into Pamplona was my worst day. The problems with my feet flared (plantar fasciitis), and every step was torture. I took a rest day and made some changes. I got new insoles, which helped a lot. I cut my miles per day way down to 5–6 miles and incrementally built back up to 10–12. I bussed or taxied across large city sections with miles of concrete and asphalt, which was hard on my feet. Anyway, take some time and evaluate the changes you need to make physically and mentally to make your Camino your Camino. I got stronger and more resilient and finished strong and cherish my time spent on the CF.

You got this! Take your time. I spent two or three days in Pamplona when I arrived; remember, it's your Camino, and listen to your body and mind. When available, I would do an 8–10 km day to ease my way into the difficulty of walking daily.

Andrea, I got to Pamplona last night and felt EXACTLY like you. My advice: take a rest day now. Please get a private room somewhere. Rest, sleep, and privacy have worked their magic on me, and I am excited to start walking again tomorrow. Those first few days are SO challenging, and our bodies are not used to this sustained effort. Give yourself a break and see how you feel in a day. (Also, feel free to reach out to me at any point—I am only a day ahead of you and will be doing shorter days for the next few days because I am learning to listen to my body. For now, that means shorter days. So it's likely we will end up in the same place at some point.) BTW, you just crossed the PYRENEES!!! What an accomplishment! That's a significant mountain range!

You can make it. It gets more and more beautiful, and remember, you have choices! Take Rest Days! Split some days up! Your Camino. Your way! Trust me, if I can do it, anyone can!

You can do it, Andrea! That one long, hard day is behind you now. Ultreia!

You are in the first week when you are getting stronger and physically active. Never quit on a bad day; wait until the next day, and you might feel like continuing on one more day. If you need to take a break, do it. If you need to take a taxi, do it. Whatever it takes because the feeling of walking into Santiago is so Epic. Good luck.

One step at a time, rest when you need to, and stop when you need to. Remember, it's the journey that is what matters most!

Boy. I can identify. My first Camino, my daughter and I got to Astoria wiped out. We had lost our camera. We were overheated. We had gotten off the trail and had blisters. She had significant hip pain following her recent surgery. We were a mess. We had to hitchhike to get across the bridge into the town because it was for cars only and not pedestrians! We were crying and thought we needed to quit. But we decided to stay in a 5-star hotel, pamper ourselves, and see if we could regroup. We did. And we finished. If we could do it, I know you can!

I recall being told, very wisely, that it is not a race. It is a Pilgrimage and opportunity to journey into yourself—one step at a time. Ignore the suggested stops. Take shorter days, sit by a stream, enjoy under the trees, and go within.

Have faith in yourself. Remember the Winnie the Pooh quote: "You're braver than you believe, stronger than you seem, & smarter than you think." You CAN do it!! Buen Camino.

There is something called trail legs. After the first 4–5 days, your body will be conditioned to what you are doing. Keep going. It's a lot of stress on the body, but your body and you will adjust. After my first week, I started moving well. The first week was hard. Just one day at a time, one step at a time. Just think about the right now and decide to walk just that day. You can figure out the tomorrow later.

In all, I received 130 comments, each filled with validation, encouragement, kindness, and helpful advice. Reading through them, I came to the realization that I could indeed overcome the challenges ahead—and part of that journey was going to involve having the courage to ask for help. The valuable lesson of seeking assistance when it's needed is something I have brought back home with me, and I continue to practice it daily.

CHAPTER 7:

The Journey There →

There are various routes to reach Saint-Jean—considered the official starting point of the French Way—depending on where you're coming from. When I did the Camino, I traveled from San Francisco, California. Chances are, if you are coming from the United States, you will have a similar journey.

I traveled from the West Coast to Saint-Jean, and this was my itinerary:

1. Fly to Madrid

2. Take the subway from Madrid Airport to Madrid Puerta de Atocha Station

- You'll want to take the Cercanías commuter train, which departs every 15 minutes from downstairs at the airport terminal (Duration: 30 minutes; cost: 5 euros).

3. Take the train from Madrid Puerta de Atocha Station to Pamplona Station

- Purchase a train ticket from Madrid Puerta de Atocha station to Pamplona station (Duration: 3 hours; cost: 113 euros).
- The train usually departs from the lower level, and you'll need to pass through a security check before accessing the platform (liquids are allowed).

4. Travel from Pamplona to Saint-Jean (Bus or Taxi)

- A daily bus departs from Pamplona station to Saint-Jean. Alternatively, if the timing doesn't align, you can find a line of people outside waiting for taxis.
- Many individuals you see with backpacks are likely fellow Pilgrims. Consider inquiring if they're heading to Saint-Jean and offering to share a cab with them if they are. The cost for a taxi there is around 110 euros, credit cards accepted, so sharing is a great money-saver, but it's also an exciting start to your Camino, allowing you to share the initial experience with fellow travelers.

CHAPTER 8

Itinerary Suggestions and Inspirations →

There are all sorts of lodgings along the Camino, from hotels with private rooms to hostels with bunk beds. Following are all the places that I booked along the Way, and for the most part, I was pleased with what I got.

I'm so glad that I overcame my early reservations about booking accommodations in advance and using a luggage transfer service. I was afraid doing those things made me a "bad" Pilgrim, but ultimately I recognized that these decisions were essential for creating the Camino experience I desired. As my book title says, *Go Your Own Way*. Well, I did it My Way—and I am so grateful that I embraced that motto. (I was *especially* grateful for it when I heard tales of fellow Pilgrims racing to secure a bed in a village by leaving at 4:00 a.m. and practically sprinting to their next destination. I knew that wasn't for me.)

Undertaking 500 miles of walking is a formidable task, even under optimal circumstances, and my chosen approach worked well for me. Next, you'll find my itinerary, along with daily reflections and quotes intended to inspire you. Unless stated otherwise, all reservations were made through Booking.com and had Wi-Fi.

ACCOMMODATIONS

Securing reservations for thirty-eight nights when you're staying somewhere new almost every one of those nights can indeed be a daunting task. When navigating the reservation process, it's crucial to consider several key factors.

1. Mileage between accommodations

When planning your daily walks—and nightly destinations—consider your fitness level and how much ground you're comfortable covering each day. Do your homework too, because you'll be covering some diverse terrain, and there will be days when you'll be expending more effort to cover a shorter distance.

2. Number of consecutive walking days before a rest day

Determine the number of days you plan to walk consecutively before taking a rest day. This decision can impact your overall pace and energy levels.

3. Location of accommodation in relation to the Camino trail

The proximity of your chosen accommodation to the Camino trail is crucial for convenience. Assess whether the places you're looking at align with your preferred walking route.

4. Reviews by other Pilgrims

Reviews from fellow Pilgrims offer valuable insights into the quality of accommodations. Don't just take my word for it; consider the experiences of others to ensure you're making informed decisions.

5. Amenities at the accommodation

Take note of amenities—in particular, laundry facilities, on-site restaurants, air-conditioning (especially during warmer months), and pools, which can be delightful bonuses to your experience.

I strongly suggest carefully weighing all these factors as you book lodging for your journey. Taking into account both your physical capabilities and personal preferences as you plan your itinerary will result in a more enjoyable Camino experience—and isn't that the point?

DAY BY DAY

Arrival day(s)

Saint-Jean-Pied-de-Port

Maison Simonenia (2 nights)

12 Rue de la Citadelle, 64220 Saint-Jean-Pied-de-Port, France

+33 5 59 37 56 10

$179

Amenities: Private bedroom with bathroom, TV, air-conditioning, dining room, breakfast

Daily thought: *You've made it. You're here!*

After all the careful planning, I've finally arrived in Saint-Jean-Pied-de-Port, France. The hotel is situated in a delightful part of Saint-Jean, just a block away from the Pilgrim's office. I'm delighted that I opted to spend two nights in this charming little town, allowing myself the time to unwind from the journey and immerse myself in the Pilgrim mindset. The memory of arriving at the Pamplona station, stepping outside, and spotting that first group of people with backpacks and hiking poles—my fellow Pilgrims—will be forever etched in my mind, as will hearing myself say (for the first of what will be hundreds of times), *"Buen Camino."* Was I nervous? Yes, but I quickly connected with the Pilgrims who shared the cab here with me. Although there's still a bit of nervousness, I find comfort in the fact that I'm not alone. My adventure has officially begun.

> **Camino Message:**
> *"A journey of a thousand miles
> begins with a single step."*
> —LAO TZU

DAY 1:
Saint-Jean-Pied-de-Port to Orisson—8.4 km/5.2 mi

Auberge Orisson

64220 Uhart-Cize

+33 6 38 26 97 38

$115.94 (Booked directly at www.refuge-orisson.com)

Amenities: Special Pilgrim dinner, breakfast, and shared bathroom

***Note:** If you desire your own space, Refuge Orisson offers two modest private chalets—essentially small structures furnished with a bed and a nightstand, boasting an incredible view of the mountain range. But since there are only two, you will need to book them in advance!

Daily thought: *You don't have to suffer.*

Day 1 presented me with a choice: ascend and cross the Pyrenees to reach the suggested stop of Roncesvalles, or linger in the Pyrenees itself. I've opted for the latter, and I'm glad I did. After all, how often does one get to spend a night in the midst of a vast mountain range? While assessing the distance in advance, I had a hunch that I could cover the walk to Roncesvalles in a single day. However, with the overarching goal of reaching Santiago in mind, I tried to make choices aimed at ensuring my success. There was no need to just plow ahead.

The moment of reaching the mountain's summit today remains vivid in my mind. Just as I was contemplating putting a halt to my walk, I turned a corner and laid eyes on my destination: Refuge Orisson. Its expansive outdoor deck was abuzz with contented Pilgrims indulging in food, drink, and the breathtaking panoramic views.

My decision to stop here has proven to be the right one, as Refuge Orisson is turning out to be the perfect inaugural haven along this extensive trail. Describing it as merely an accommodation for Pilgrims arriving by foot from Saint-Jean-Pied-de-Port doesn't capture the essence of this place. It is much more than that. Without divulging the specifics that make it truly unforgettable, let's just say that, as an introvert concerned about meeting people, Refuge Orisson facilitated connections with fellow Pilgrims whom I suspect will accompany me on this journey to the very end.

Meanwhile, the view through my little wooden chalet's picture window of the sky and the valley below is nothing short of breathtaking. If this is a glimpse of what the Camino holds in store for me, this is going to be an extraordinary adventure!

Camino Message
"Walking is man's best medicine."
—HIPPOCRATES

DAY 2:

Orisson to Roncesvalles—15.6 km/9.7 mi

La Posada de Roncesvalles

Carretera N-135, s/n, Calle Ntra. Sra. de Roncesvalles, 2, 31650 Roncesvalles, Navarra, Spain

+34 948 79 03 22

$88 (Booked directly at https://laposada.roncesvalles.es/?lang=en)

Amenities: Private bedroom with bathroom and bathtub, TV, restaurant serving breakfast and dinner

Daily thought: *It's okay to pee outside.*

Do I like to go to the bathroom outside? No. Do I occasionally get the squat angle wrong and pee on my shoe? Yes. But you know what, I feel better every time I just tell myself to stop and go, rather than hold it in and pray for a rest stop ahead. You don't have to have a penis to pee outside. Was that too straightforward? I apologize. Let me rephrase: it's perfectly acceptable for women to go to the bathroom outside. If nature calls, answer it. The sensation of holding it in and walking, for me at least, stirs up a chaotic swirl of anxiety and questions: *How far until the next café? When will I reach a town? Am I going to have an accident?* So, as of today, I've adopted a new mantra: "Stay hydrated. Use nature's restroom. It's perfectly fine. Everyone does it."

Camino Message

*"Everywhere is within walking distance
if you have the time."*
—STEVEN WRIGHT

DAY 3:

Roncesvalles to Zubiri—21.4 km/13.3 mi

Casa Rural Txantxorena

5 Calle la Zatoya, 31630 Zubiri, Spain

+34 679 12 93 96

$100

Amenities: Private bedroom with bathroom, laundry, hot tub, packed lunch, lounge with fireplace, garden, cafeteria

Daily thought: *Always bring food.*

As it is just me walking, I notice that my thoughts are frequently preoccupied with the concern of whether I have enough food. While there have always seemed to be numerous establishments where food is available so far, I am mindful that there may be stretches ahead that will not offer quite so many options. So, I must always ensure I have sustenance in my backpack.

Last time I traveled the Camino with my friend Gladys, she told me that anytime a hotel or albergue has a buffet, I should prepare myself a sandwich and a snack to take with me for the day. And you know what? Every time I take a break, I am so thrilled to see that food in my pack. So, keeping that in mind, I acquired two small containers, and this morning I stocked up on provisions from the Casa Rural's breakfast buffet before heading out. Knowing that I won't have to fret about finding a place to eat has alleviated some of my anxiety about successfully completing this incredible trek today, tomorrow, and the next day. Santiago, here I come.

> **Camino Message**
> *"Don't come to the Camino looking for answers. Instead, come with an open heart, and you may be surprised by what you find."*
> —JANE V. BLANCHARD

DAY 4:
Zubiri to Pamplona—20.4 km /12.7 mi

Hotel Sancho Ramirez

11, Bajo, 31008 Pamplona, Spain

+34 948 27 17 12

$90

Amenities: Private bedroom with bathroom, TV, air-conditioning, restaurant and bar, lounge with TV and board games, buffet breakfast

Daily thought: *Asking for help, even virtually, is essential.* Today happened to be my most arduous day of walking. My spirits were low, and I grappled with a sense of making no progress at all. The extreme weather fluctuations, from a morning downpour to an afternoon of scorching sun, may have played a role. Additionally, my hotel, located in the farthest corner of town, didn't serve dinner until 7:30, adding to my emotional exhaustion. As I sank into bed twenty minutes ago, I felt drained in body, mind, and spirit, and doubts about my ability started creeping in. Unsure of what to do, I reached for my iPad and connected with a supportive online community for women on the Camino called the Camigas—and almost immediately, the responses started pouring in. Their kind words have encouraged me to approach this journey one day at a time. I find solace in that perspective. And isn't this ability to lift each other up what makes women unique? I think so. I am so grateful for this connection with my sister Pilgrims. I have a feeling it's going to play a huge role in helping me make it to the finish line.

DAY 5:

Pamplona to Puenta Ła Reina – 23.9 km/15 mi

Hotel Jakue

Calle Irunbidea, 34, Puente la Reina

+34 948 34 10 17

$108

Amenities: Private bedroom with bathroom and bathtub, air-conditioning, seating area, restaurant serving breakfast and dinner, bar, packed lunches upon request, elevator, twenty-four-hour reception desk

Daily thought: *Take care of your feet.*

On this third day, I noticed a couple of blisters emerging on my feet, prompting the realization that I needed to make some adjustments. So I once again sought advice from my fellow Pilgrims, and the most consistent recommendation I got was to apply Vaseline to my feet three times a day: in the morning before I start out, during my midday break, and before bed. They also emphasized changing my socks midday. The best news? Vaseline is sold at most stores, supermarkets, and even tiny little corner stores on the Camino, so I'll be able to implement this advice right away. I extend my gratitude to those wonderful Pilgrims, with a special thank-you from my soon-to-be rejuvenated feet!

> **Camino Message**
> *"All truly great thoughts are conceived by walking."*
> —FRIEDRICH NIETZSCHE

DAY 6:

Puenta la Reina to Estella—21.6 km/13.4 mi

Hostal El Volante

Merkatondoa, 2, 31200 Estella, Spain

+34 625 37 97 68

$70

Amenities: Private bedroom with bathroom, TV, laundry, central heating, air-conditioning upon request, free bicycle storage, elevator, laundry, restaurant serving breakfast and dinner

Daily thoughts: *Take care of your body.*

It happened: I got sick today. And this wasn't just a case of troublesome sinuses; my intestines decided to join in on the chaos, which meant I had to be vigilant about finding cafés, bars, and restaurants with bathroom facilities along the way. (Relying on nature's privacy was out of the question, as there was not a tree or building in sight.) In retrospect, maybe I should have considered cutting my walk short and taking a taxi the rest of the way, but I pulled a Forrest Gump and just forged ahead. Fortunately, I found several places along my route where I was able to grab refreshments, eat, and, most crucially, use the bathroom.

Where I come from, you can't just walk into a business and use their restroom without making a purchase. Today, as I was reaching the end of my walk, I suddenly realized I desperately needed a restroom—and my albergue was all the way on the other side of town. In that moment, two thoughts raced through my mind: *There is no way I'll make it to my hotel,* and *I need absolute privacy.* The problem—I was walking through a wide, open space with no trees, surrounded by fellow Pilgrims.

With laser-like focus, I spotted a solitary building at the town's edge—a hostel. Sweat trickled down my forehead and my stomach tightened. I prayed the building had a bathroom, and I would be allowed to use it. I beelined through the front door, where I was presented with a check-in desk and an adjoining bathroom. The desk clerk was on the phone, so I seized the opportunity to use the bathroom. Aware of what was about to happen, I immediately turned on the faucet to drown out any sounds.

I have never felt greater relief.

Afterward, feeling both relief and embarrassment, I came out to the check-in office and offered the clerk some money. He just smiled and said, "We are all human."

Amen to that. The Camino truly provided today.

My takeaway from this ordeal is to *listen to your body*. It's constantly sending signals, and especially while walking the Camino, it's crucial that you pay attention and respond to those messages.

Thank you, kind soul, for allowing me to use the bathroom!

Camino Message

"We all want progress, but if you're
on the wrong road, progress means doing
an about-turn and walking back to the
right road; in that case, the man who turns
back soonest is the most progressive."
—C. S. LEWIS

DAY 7:

Estella to Los Arcos—21.5 km/13.3 mi

Apartamentos Jurramendi–Los Arcos
Calle Mayor 69, 31210 Los Arcos, Spain
+34 650 11 43 78
$93

Amenities: Studios and one-, two-, or three-bedroom apartments, private bathroom, bathtub upon request, TV, laundry, and kitchen equipped with an oven, microwave, toaster, refrigerator, and coffee machine

Daily thought: *If you can, get your own place to stay.*
Today, for some reason, was what I can only describe as brutal. It might be due to the lingering effects of my illness, but physically I had no choice but to take breaks—many, many breaks—on my walk today, which made the day feel incredibly long. So I can't help but feel overjoyed right now by the fact that tonight I have my very own apartment, equipped with all the lovely modern-day amenities I could possibly want: living room, kitchen, dining room, laundry. Having that feeling of "being home" (even though it isn't technically home) is such a relief. I don't know about you, but when I'm sick there is nowhere else that I want to be more than home.

Having my own apartment tonight means I didn't have to worry about arranging meals for today and tomorrow when I arrived this evening. Instead, I just strolled a couple of blocks to a grocery store to stock up on supplies and strolled on back home.

It truly is comforting as well as rejuvenating to have your own space. You can wash and dry your clothes, prepare your own meals, walk around in your pj's.

Tonight, those small comforts have provided me with just what I needed to feel better in body, mind, and soul.

> **Camino Message**
> *"Walk slow, don't rush. That place*
> *you have to reach is yourself."*
> —José Ortega y Gasset

DAY 8:

Los Arcos to Logroño—27.8 km/17.3 mi

Hotel Gran Via

Gran Vía Juan Carlos I, 71 bis, 26005 Logroño, Spain

+34 941 28 78 50

$89

Amenities: Private bedroom with bathroom, bathtub upon request, TV, air-conditioning, elevator, buffet breakfast, snack bar serving light meals and drinks

Daily thought: *Slow down.*

After spending the entire day walking through the peaceful countryside, I arrived this evening in the bustling city of Logroño. And I have to say, the sudden transition from being surrounded by serene farm fields to the lively atmosphere of a big city felt overwhelming. Imagine yourself in the state of New York, starting off the day walking through the apple orchards of the Catskills to suddenly being thrown into the New Year's Eve ball drop at Times Square. It's a genuine shock to the system. I have always loved that movie expression, "I've a feeling we're not in Kansas anymore," and that is how I felt: as if I had suddenly found myself not on the Camino.

I quickly realized that for my own well-being, I needed to slow down in that moment and to remain mindful of both myself and my belongings. The combination of fatigue and the overwhelming buzz of the urban environment I'd found myself in made for prime conditions for me to lose things—and, for some reason, to feel my emotional floodgates open. Maybe it was the feeling of being back in something that more closely resembled my version of the "real world," but a wave of yearning for my loved ones overcame me, and I found myself wondering if I really even wanted to continue walking.

Just slow down, I reminded myself again. And funnily enough, as soon as I made that decision, I looked around me and began to spot Pilgrims sprinkled around the town square—in cafés, in front of albergues. I was still on the Camino, just in a different form.

As soon as I accepted that notion, that feeling of having to guard my things became much less urgent. I mean, really, who wants to steal dirty clothes from an unwashed, messy-haired, fifty-eight-year-old Pilgrim in Birkenstocks?

Camino Message

"It is your road and yours alone. Others may walk with you, but no one can walk it for you."
—Rumi

DAY 9:
Logroño to Ventosa—20.34 km/12.64 mi

Hotel Rural Las Águedas
Plaza de Santa Coloma, 11, 26371 Ventosa, Spain
+34 636 22 06 29
$86

Amenities: Private bedroom with bathroom, TV, outside patio, lawn, and lounge area with barbecue, delicious homemade dinner for guests, spacious inside lounge with TV, board games, and a library

Daily thought: *Prebooking has its benefits.*

After a lengthy day of traversing vineyards and fields, staying here at Hotel Rural Las Águedas is a true delight. As described on the website, the hotel is an eighteenth-century farmhouse meticulously renovated to offer modern and comfortable amenities. The thoughtful decor seamlessly blends period furniture and antiques with a modern, vibrant atmosphere, conjuring the charm of bygone eras.

With only six rooms, the atmosphere at Las Águedas is intimate and the hospitality is akin to being among family. From the lovely living room to the elegant dining room, I feel as if I'm staying in a home—a home made with love for traveling Pilgrims.

After I settled in earlier, a Pilgrim's dream unfolded: Dinner was served promptly at 6:30. The food was already on the table when I walked into the room, and all I could think when I saw it was, *This must be what heaven looks like.* In the formal dining room, we were treated to a delightful homemade three-course meal: a lush green salad with nuts and fruit and paella for dinner, a delectable local pudding for dessert, all complemented by bottles of wine from a nearby region. The whole experience—sitting at a dining room table, savoring a delicious meal served on hand-painted china with fellow Pilgrims, and then retiring to my bedroom at a relatively early hour—made me feel as if I were being given a giant hug.

Tonight's evening of incredible food and fun conversation—plus the promise of a restful sleep to come—is exactly what this Pilgrim girl needed. Sure, not everyone may believe in prebooking, but for me it's transformed reaching Santiago from a possibility to a probability. My gas tank just went from empty to full.

Camino Message
*"In every walk with nature,
one receives more than he seeks."*
—JOHN MUIR

DAY 10:

Ventosa to Santo Domingo de la Calzada—
29.4 km/18.2 mi

El Molino de Floren

Calle Margubete 5, 26250 Santo Domingo de
la Calzada, Spain

+34 941 34 29 31

$55

Amenities: Private bedroom with bathroom,
TV, patio, buffet breakfast, gift shop

Daily thought: *Having a restaurant on site can be a
total lifesaver.*

After a delightful walk today, punctuated by a stop to
appreciate the beauty of Monasterio de Santa Maria, my
excitement grew as I reached my destination, El Molino
de Floren—an establishment that has truly lived up to
its promise. Nestled in a renovated water mill from
the nineteenth century, El Molino boasts ten spacious
rooms, a cozy living room, an inviting dining room, and
an outdoor patio.

This charming spot also provides two of the services
I've come to value most on the Camino: a clean, comfortable bedroom and an excellent restaurant. I've really
come to appreciate the luxury of staying in a place that
provides access to food. There are times when the search
for an eatery can be way too time-consuming, so knowing there will be a restaurant on site at the end of my day
is a valuable gift, saving me both time and effort. Who
needs to experience "where will I eat tonight" panic on a
journey like this one?

Camino Message
*"Use the guides and the maps to lead
you to Santiago; use the lessons learned on
the Camino to find your way."*
—JANE V. BLANCHARD

DAY 11:
Santo Domingo de la Calzada to Belorado— 21.8 km/13.5 mi

Hotel Jacobeo

Avenida de Burgos 3, 09250 Belorado, Spain

+34 947 58 00 10

$97

Amenities: Private bedroom with bathroom and bathtub, TV, elevator, air-conditioning, laundry, coffee house on site, breakfast buffet

Daily thought: *Having something go wrong does not have to be a catastrophe. It's all about how you respond to the challenge.*

Each day you walk the Camino, you are presented with challenges, from finding sustenance to finding lodging. Just as in life, unexpected things happen, and I have found over these last eleven days that when things go sideways, the only thing I can control is my emotional response. So, the first thing I do is take a slow, deep breath in and let a slow, deep breath out. I may even repeat this a couple of times. Once I've calmed down, I ask myself, *How big is this problem, and do I need help?* Nine times out of ten, the problem is not as big as it seems, and by just taking a moment, I quickly begin to see solutions (typically, this involved asking a fellow Pilgrim for advice and/or help).

Yes, the Camino provides.

Camino Message

"You have brains in your head. You have feet in your shoes. You can steer yourself in any direction you choose."
—Dr. Seuss

DAY 12:

Belorado to Villafranca Montes de Oca—11.1 km/6.9 mi

Hotel San Antón Abad

Hospital, 4, 09257 Villafranca-Montes de Oca, Spain

+34 947 58 21 50

$96

Amenities: Private bedroom with bathroom, bathtub upon request, suites offer a seating area, restaurant offering a set-menu dinner (six starters and six main dishes to choose from) and buffet breakfast, twenty-four-hour reception

Daily thought: *Be grateful.*

Taking a rest day at a former hospital turned out to be quite a unique experience. Last night (my plan-B night because I made a mistake in my booking), I stayed in the Pilgrim community room. Tonight, I've found myself in a luxurious suite with a living room, bathtub, and a bed fit for a queen, super-soft sheets and all. I'm so lucky to have been able to spend not one but two nights here. I got to experience what many Pilgrims do on their trip and then got to luxuriate in my own private space. I also gave myself a break and took a rest day!

In my usual one-night stays at various properties, I often don't get to see all the hardworking individuals who make walking the Camino possible. No one has just one job here; everyone seems to wear multiple hats—receptionist, hostess, server, cleaner. I realize that as tired and hungry Pilgrims, waiting for our rooms or to order food can be frustrating. Yet, every single day, an entirely new group of Pilgrims arrives with the exact same needs and pretty much the same questions. And here are all these generous individuals, working so hard to take care of me, a total stranger.

Without these generous folks, there is absolutely no way I would ever make it to Santiago. I am sincerely grateful for each one of them. So, the moral of this story? Cultivate patience, practice gratitude, and strive to be the Pilgrim you want to be—oh, and always double-check your reservations.

> **Camino Message**
> *"Walking brings me back to myself."*
> —LAURETTE MORTIMER

DAY 13:
Villafranca Montes de Oca to Burgos—
34.4 km/21.4 mi

Abba Burgos
Fernán González, 72, 09003 Burgos, Spain
+34 947 00 11 00
San Juan de Ortega
$148

Amenities: Private bedroom with bathroom, TV, heated indoor swimming pool, sauna, gym, paddle tennis court, café-bar, room service, twenty-four-hour reception, laundry, ironing, dry-cleaning services, restaurant serving fresh seasonal dishes and buffet breakfast

Daily thought: *Cities have lots of services.*
Being back in a big city presents the perfect opportunity to take advantage of all the available services—restaurants, laundromats, grocery stores, and more.

After checking in to Abba Burgos this evening, my first stop was the laundromat conveniently situated near a restaurant and a supermarket. Thankfully, the machines have timers and locks, which means I was able to use that time to grab a bite to eat and do some grocery shopping. I love when I can be efficient.

Certainly, in a bustling city filled with people beyond just Pilgrims, it's necessary to slow down and be more mindful. However, the upside is that Burgos offers a wealth of services not found in the smaller villages. After completing my chores, I plan to return to my hotel for a refreshing swim, a relaxing sauna, and an early bedtime.

The Camino has a way of reminding us how the simple things in life can bring immense pleasure. I hope I remember this back home. What is it that I really need? Not much.

> **Camino Message**
> *"If you're in a bad mood, go for a walk. Go for another walk if you are still in a bad mood."*
> —HIPPOCRATES

DAY 14:
Burgos to Tarjados—11.8 km/7.4 mi

La Casa de Beli

Avenida General Yagüe Nº 16, 09130 Tardajos, Spain

+34 629 351 675

$60

Amenities: Private bedroom with bathroom, TV, restaurant, terrace, views of the garden, ATM, bike storage, massage services

Daily thought: *Short days are good.*

Scheduling a "short walk day" turned out to be a delightful decision. With no sense of urgency, I took my time checking out of the hotel this morning. A leisurely buffet breakfast and an excellent, unhurried stretching and meditation session in my room set the tone for the day. Typically, I've been experiencing a sense of urgency to start walking, a mental nudge telling me each morning, *Okay, you need to get ready and get going.* Today, knowing that I didn't have far to go allowed me to experience true calm. I didn't have to focus solely on reaching my destination; instead, I could savor and enjoy every step of the journey. Honestly, after all the big days I've been doing, 7.4 miles really felt like just a stroll down the block.

> ### Camino Message
> *"An early-morning walk is a blessing for the whole day."*
> —HENRY DAVID THOREAU

DAY 15:
Tardajos to Hontanas—21.6 km/13.42 mi

Hotel Villa Fontanas
23 Calle Real, 09227 Hontanas, Spain
+34 680 29 62 38
$66

Amenities: Private bedroom with bathroom, TV, washer and dryer

Daily thought: *You must protect your feet and your skin.* Every day, I am learning how to better take care of myself. Today's lessons have turned out to be focused on my physical well-being—the health of my feet, knees, and skin.

First, I've learned that if there is a choice between walking on hard cobblestone versus soft green grass, the grass is the way to go. When you're walking all day, every day, this can make such a difference in how much wear and tear you put on your body. Second, I've found that wrapping myself in a lightweight scarf has the dual function of helping me stay cooler and protecting my skin from the sun. There are certain things that are avoidable, and one of those things is sunburn. Walking the Camino is challenging enough without adding the discomfort of sunburn to the list.

Every time I remembered to apply these lessons today, I could feel my body experiencing an immediate sense of relaxation, grateful for the care it was receiving. When you're asking so much of your body, it's important to nurture it in return.

Camino Message
"If you listen to your body when it whispers, you won't have to hear it scream."
—CHEROKEE PROVERB

DAY 16:
Hontanas to Boadilla del Camino—27.3 km/17 mi

Hotel Rural en El Camino

Calle del Rosario, 1, 34468 Boadilla del Camino, Spain

+34 979 81 09 99

$60

Amenities: Private bedroom with bathroom, TV, elevator, bar, shared lounge, terrace, and Italian breakfast

Daily thought: *Thank goodness I made reservations.* The good news: more and more people are walking the Camino. The bad news: more and more people are walking the Camino.

I would love to live in a world where *everyone* could experience the magic of the Camino. But accommodations on the Camino are filling up faster than ever these days, and that means many Pilgrims are being told "there's no room at the inn" at the end of a long, grueling day of walking. So, each morning, regardless of where you are staying, you will feel an energy shift as the Pilgrims around you feel they must get up and out incredibly early to race to the next location just to get a bed for the night. This also means that often they miss out on the joy of the day's walk.

Sure, I've faced lots of challenges on this journey—but finding a bed has not been one of them, and for that I am grateful. Some may say, "It's not very Pilgrim-like to make reservations," but I am glad I listened to my inner voice telling me to do what works best for me as I prepared for this trip.

> **Camino Message**
> *"Walk with the knowledge that
> you are never alone."*
> —Audrey Hepburn

DAY 17:

Boadilla del Camino to Frómista—5.9 km/3.66 mi

Hotel Rural San Pedro
Avenida del Ejército Español, 8, 34440
Frómista, Spain
+34 979 810 016
$65

Amenities: Private bedroom with bathroom, elevator, Pilgrim buffet breakfast

Daily thought: *Don't believe everything you read.*

It wasn't a catastrophic situation, but it certainly wasn't a pleasant experience. The hotel I stayed at today had touted laundry service on its website. However, my host clarified that the description was not entirely accurate, stating, "We do not have laundry service, and there are no laundromats anywhere in town." Fortunately, I had one more set of clean underwear left, but going forward, I've learned the importance of confirming such amenities in advance! I don't want to offend other Pilgrims with my stinky clothes, but more importantly I don't want to offend myself.

> **Camino Message**
> *"When you follow the crowd,*
> *you lose yourself, but when you follow*
> *your soul, you lose the crowd."*
> —Anonymous

DAY 18:

Frómista to Carrión de los Condes—19.3 km/12 mi

Hotel Real Monasterio de San Zoilo

Obispo Souto, s/n, 34120 Carrión de los
Condes, Spain

+34 979 88 00 50

$83

Amenities: Private and shared rooms (the building is a former monastery, and the private bedrooms have a rustic feel—some even have four-poster beds); bathtub, air-conditioning, heating, and TV available to private rooms upon request; restaurant serving traditional Spanish dishes made from local produce and a daily breakfast buffet; chapel (make a request to see it!)

Daily thought: *Walking and talking can make for a pleasant day.*

Today, I had the delightful experience of reconnecting with a college friend, Kristin, during my walk. It served as a vivid reminder of the joy that comes from walking and talking in good company. The day seemed to pass in the blink of an eye! While I've spent numerous enjoyable days walking solo, I now recognize the value of having a walking companion from time to time. I imagine other Pilgrims might share this same feeling. Although I cherish my solitude—those contemplative walking moments where you get to go deep inside your own mind—Kristin's company highlighted the beauty of forging connections. I think I will reach out on the Camigas page to see if anyone wants to walk with me tomorrow.

Camino Message
*"I don't know where I'm going,
but I am on my way."*
—VOLTAIRE

DAY 19:

Carrión de los Condes to Ledigos – 23.1 km/14.35 mi

Albergue La Morena
Calle Carretera, 3, 34347 Ledigos, Spain
+34 626 97 21 18
$60
Amenities: Private bedrooms with bathrooms, restaurant, bar, washer and dryer, restaurant serving Pilgrim dinner and continental breakfast

Daily thought: *It's okay to ask questions.*

Staying at Hotel Real Monasterio reminded me of an important lesson: if you are unsure of something, ask. Until now, I have been intimidated about asking questions at the places I stay. I often won't say anything at all, in fact, because I am embarrassed that I have such limited Spanish. But this morning, as I was getting ready to check out, I ran into a Pilgrim friend who asked me if I had seen the chapel at the hotel. I said no, and she said, "You must see it. Just ask at the front desk."

I took her advice—and ended up using the opportunity to ask not only about the chapel but also about something even more important to me: the possibility of getting breakfast. (Food seems to be always top of mind these days!). I soon learned that both access to the private chapel and eating at the breakfast buffet were included in my reservation. Neither amenity had been mentioned at check-in, so I realized I need to forget my awkward discomfort and ask questions. After all, I can always use Google Translate or ask a Spanish-speaking Pilgrim to help me out if the person I'm asking doesn't speak English. Imagine that—asking for help when I need it! What a concept.

Camino Message
"It's supposed to be hard.
If it wasn't hard, everyone would do it.
The hard is what makes it great."
—TOM HANKS, *A LEAGUE OF THEIR OWN*

DAY 20:
Ledigos to Sahagún—14.8 km/9.2 mi

Domus Viatoris

Carretera Sahagun-Arriondas, s/n, 24320

Sahagún, Spain

+34 679 97 78 28

$44

Amenities: Private bedroom with bathroom, TV, laundry, souvenir shop, terrace, bar, restaurant serving characteristic dishes from the Castilla region and continental breakfast

Daily thought: *It's perfectly fine to take your dirty laundry out of your bag at check-in!*

I don't know about you, but every now and then I do something and have an *aha* moment, wondering why I hadn't been doing it sooner. Today was one of those situations for me. Whenever I check into a new place, I typically inquire about laundry services. More often than not, my room ends up located on the top floor of the building while the laundry facilities are on the ground floor, with no elevator in sight. Consequently, I must lug my entire bags upstairs to my room, unpack the dirty clothes, and then haul them back downstairs. After a day of extensive walking, this routine can be quite exhausting.

And then, today, inspiration struck: instead of trekking up the stairs with my heavy bag, I decided to drop off my dirty clothes on the ground floor first. Not only did this mean I ascended to my room carrying a much more manageable load, it also gave me a head start on other Pilgrims checking in who had laundry to do. I can't lie, I love getting my laundry done first!

Camino Message
*"I was never going to go if I waited
for someone to come with me."*
—Anonymous

DAY 21:

Sahagún to Bercionas del Real Camino – 13.2 km/8.2 mi

Hostal Rivero

Calle Mayor, 12, Bercianos del Real Camino

+34 987 78 42 87

$48 (Booked directly at

www.hostalrivero99.wixsite.com)

Amenities: Private bedroom with bathroom,
TV, restaurant

Daily thought: *Wow, I am strong.*

Today unfolded as a pleasant and relaxed day, particularly significant as it marks the twenty-first day of my journey. In every aspect—mentally, physically, and emotionally—I feel a heightened sense of strength. Reflecting on my daily mileage, I can't help but appreciate the realization that I'm framing it as *I had to walk "only" 8.2 miles today.* My fellow Camigas predicted this shift, and indeed, 8 miles now feels like a minor feat. What a difference a few days make!

Camino Message

"The earth has music for those who listen."
—WILLIAM SHAKESPEARE

DAY 22:

**Bercianos del Real Camino to Mansilla de las Mulas—
26.7km/16.7 mi**

La Casa de Mansilla

Plaza del Pozo 11, 24210 Mansilla de las Mulas,
Spain

1-888-861-8331

$81

Amenities: Full one-bedroom apartment with private bathroom, TV, washing machine, dining area, fully equipped kitchen, balcony with city views, bathtub upon request

Daily thought: *Kitchens are incredible.*

On this twenty-second day, if asked about my primary challenge right now, it would be the noticeable absence of vegetables in my diet. While I thoroughly enjoy a bocadillo, there comes a time when I crave more than just meat, cheese, and bread. Fortunately, having an apartment with a kitchen tonight has allowed me to address this issue. I loaded up on essentials like fruits and vegetables at the store this afternoon—and despite my lack of culinary expertise, the dinner I made myself (steamed vegetables and salad) proved to be exactly what I needed. To me, it was a five-star meal. And I was able to replenish my non-food supplies at the store too— Vaseline for my feet and Advil for any aches and pains to come. As a bonus, it turns out that grocery stores are a more economical option for those items compared to pharmacies! I couldn't be happier right now.

> **Camino Message**
> *"In every walk with nature,
> one receives far more than he seeks."*
> —John Muir

DAY 23:
Mansilla de las Mulas to León—18.1 km/11.2 mi

León Hotel Spa Paris
Ancha, 18, 24003 León, Spain
+34 987 23 86 00
$62

Amenities: Private bedroom with bathroom, TV, air-conditioning, elevator, spa with indoor pool, hot tub, and massages, attached restaurant and bar, packed lunches

Daily thought: There's nothing better than a spa day.
While I understand that many Pilgrims opt for a more rugged experience on the Camino, I've realized that each journey is unique and personal. Today, my experience took a different turn—a stay in a hotel with a spa—and it proved to be an incredible gift to myself at a cost of only 10 euros!

After savoring a late-afternoon meal of delectable steak tacos today, I made my way to my hotel's spa for an afternoon of luxury and body healing. I made my way through the facility's offerings—steam room, jet shower, hot tub, pool, and cold pool—and by the time I reached the last heavenly treatment (a moment of recline on a heated ceramic tile bed), I couldn't have felt more relaxed. This indulgence set the stage for a night of blissful sleep, leaving every ache and pain behind.

I have immense gratitude to Léon Hotel Spa Paris for gifting me with such a rejuvenating experience. I can't emphasize enough what a good idea it is to treat yourself to such moments of pampering along the Camino. Suffering is not required here.

Camino Message
"Methinks that the moment my legs begin to move, my thoughts begin to flow."
—HENRY DAVID THOREAU

DAY 24:
León to Villadangos del Páramo – 22.4 km/13.9 mi

Hotel Avenida III

Carretera León-Astorga, km 17, Villadangos
del Páramo

+34 987 390 311

$93

Amenities: Private bedroom with bathroom,
TV, bathtub with jets upon request, restaurant

Daily thought: *Podcasts are your friend.*

Three weeks into this journey, despite my strengthened
body, there are still moments when the path ahead seems
to stretch longer. When I'm walking solo, in the absence
of the camaraderie I've found with my new Camino
friends, I've embraced listening to podcasts during my
walks. Some might argue that it's not the traditional
Camino way—but if people can walk and talk, why
can't I listen to someone talk? The experience has been
delightful; I relish my surroundings while absorbing
intriguing information. Surprisingly, my walks now
feel shorter, and I seem to reach my destination with
astonishing speed.

(A quick note on Hotel Avenida III: Initial impressions
may be more "truck stop" than "luxury accommodation,"
but once you're in your room, the external appearance
will become inconsequential. When booking, request a
room in the newer building for the added luxury of a jetted
bathtub. Upon arrival, expect no one at the reception desk;
instead, ring the doorbell, get buzzed in, and find your
name and room key on the front desk. Leave the key there
the next day when you depart. As for dining, if the hotel's
ground-floor dining room is closed (and it may well be), a

neighboring restaurant—also not very attractive from the outside—offers surprisingly delicious food. The outside appearances of these places are not great, but they met my needs and beyond . . . especially the massage jets in the bathtub!)

Camino Message
*"When everything feels like an uphill struggle,
just think of the view from the top."*
—ANONYMOUS

DAY 25:

Villadangos del Páramo to Astorga—26.4 km/16.4 mi

Housingleón–Apartamentos Fauno
Prieto de Castro n° 2, 24700 Astorga, Spain
+34 640 96 43 52
$111
Amenities: Entire apartment with private bathroom, kitchen with refrigerator, tea/coffee maker, dining area, dining table, elevator, washing machine

Daily thought: *My feet love Vaseline and clean socks.*
It seems so long ago since those first few days of fresh blisters on my feet. Thanks to my daily application of Vaseline (morning, noon, and night) and a routine change of socks midday, my feet are in perfect shape, with no blisters.

I know everyone has different solutions for taking care of their feet, but this simple solution has worked great for me.

Camino Message
"Not all those who wander are lost."
—J. R. R. TOLKIEN

DAY 26:

Astorga to Rabanal del Camino—20.1 km/12.5 mi

Posada El Tesin

Calle Real s/n, 24722 Rabanal del Camino, Spain

+34 635 52 75 22

$66

Amenities: Private bedroom with bathroom, TV, bathtub upon request, restaurant serving continental breakfast

Daily thought: *Sometimes, you must be resourceful.*

I always book a room with a bathtub when I can. The simple act of stretching out in a hot bath rejuvenates my body, and I end up having an incredible night's sleep—which, as we know, is one of the critical elements that help the body recover after a long day's walk.

Today's accommodation had a bathtub but no tub plug, and I was told they had no plugs on site. I sense this has been done on purpose—an attempt to save water, maybe? But hey, after twenty-six days of walking, this little "glitch" was not going to set me back; after all that I've been through, I knew I could figure out a solution. My body was aching for that hot water.

I had many solutions in mind. I thought about plugging the drain with towels. I thought about using a plastic bag. But I knew that wouldn't really work; because sooner than later, the water would drain. I needed something to fit in the drain to block the water flow. *Huh,* I thought, *what do I have that seals off water?* And then it came to me: I had my wax earplugs—the kind swimmers use in open water!

I pressed the two ear plugs together, merging them into one large lump of wax, and it worked perfectly to stop the drain. Minutes later, I was luxuriating in a nice, hot, steamy bath.

That's the thing about the Camino. You come up against challenges, and it's up to you to figure out the solution. The Camino can boost your self confidence in your overall physical strength, but today's realization boosted my confidence in my *mental* strength.

Camino Message

"Pilgrimage is a symbol of life. It makes us think of life as walking, as a path. If a person does not walk but instead stays still, this is not useful; it accomplishes nothing. Think of water: when water is not in the river, it does not course, but instead it remains still and stagnates. A soul that does not walk in life doing good, doing many things that one must do for society, to assist others, or who does not walk through life seeking God and inspiration from the Holy Spirit is a soul that finishes in mediocrity and spiritual poverty. Please: do not stand still in life!"
—POPE FRANCIS

DAY 27:
Rabanal del Camino to Molinaseca—25.3 km/15.72 mi

The Way Hotel Molinaseca

El Palacio, 10, 24413 Molinaseca, Spain

+34 631 14 93 50

$51

Amenities: Private bedroom with bathroom, TV, breakfast

Daily thought: *Take it all in.*

Today was a monumental day of hiking for me, both physically and emotionally.

First, there was the physical challenge of climbing up and down the mountain. The climb itself was not terrible, as I know how to walk at my pace. The challenge for me was not about endurance but more about ability as I faced the descent, which was steep and very, very rocky.

But more than that it was an emotional day, as today's climb brought me to the Iron Cross, where you lay down the rocks you brought. This can mean different things to different people. To me, it symbolizes the laying down of burdens—both my own and those of some of my loved ones.

My two suggestions for today: (1) take your time at the Iron Cross to take in all the "feels" that may come to you, and (2) on the way down, if you think the descent is too much, do not be shy about asking at any of the cafés for them to call you a cab. I know I wish I had. But also know that if you decide to hold out and walk the entire way, there is a river in Molinaseca that can heal what aches you. Yes, the water is painfully ice cold—but that's exactly what your feet, ankles, shins, and knees need. Don't hesitate; take the plunge.

> **Camino Message**
> *"The best part of the Camino
> is the Camino."*
> —JANE V. BLANCHARD

*"The best part of the Camino
is the Camino."*
—JANE V. BLANCHARD

DAY 28:

Molinaseca to Cacabelos—19.5 km/12.12 mi

Hostal Santa Maria
C/ Santa Maria, 20, 24540 Cacabelos, Spain
+34 987 54 95 88
$54
Amenities: Private bedroom with bathroom, TV, air-conditioning, laundry, bathtub upon request

Daily thought: *If you wait, the hot water will come.*
Given the physical and emotional challenges of the previous day's walk, I opted yesterday for a leisurely pace on the trail, which meant arriving at my destination after most other Pilgrims had gotten there. Typically, this isn't an issue, since I always have a reservation. However, a complication arose last night when I found there was no hot water left for my shower. Yep—my fellow Pilgrims had gotten to it first.

Recognizing that my response to any situation is within my control, I chose to forgo the shower and wait until the morning. Interestingly, this morning, those same Pilgrims who hurried to reach town yesterday were also in a rush to depart this morning—resulting in no competition for hot water. Taking advantage of this, after a relaxed meditation and stretching session, I finally enjoyed a nice, long, hot shower. Heaven.

Camino Message
*"Don't be scared to walk alone.
Don't be scared to like it."*
—John Muir

DAY 29:

Cacabelos to Villafranca del Bierzo—7.9 km/4.9 mi

Las Doñas del Portazgo
Calle Ribadeo, 2, 24500 Villafranca del Bierzo,
León, Spain
+34 987 54 27 42
$96

Amenities: Private bedroom with bathroom with hydromassage shower, TV, twenty-four-hour reception, restaurant serving local cuisine and a varied breakfast

Daily thought: *Be present.*

As I approach the thirtieth day of my Pilgrimage, I've observed my thoughts drifting toward reaching Santiago and returning to my life back home. I've noticed a similar mindset among my fellow Pilgrims as we've reminisced about the past adventures of our journey. It became clear to me today that we must bring our minds back to the present moment. After all, today is called "the present" for a reason. We need to regroup mentally and focus on the experiences unfolding in the here and now. My Camino is not over, and I need to stay focused on taking it all in. I am here, now, and I am choosing to be present for it.

> ### Camino Message
> *"As you start to walk out on the way,
> the way appears."*
> —Rumi

DAY 30:

Villa Franca del Bierzo to Las Herrerías—19.6 km/12.2 mi

Casa Lixa

C. Cam. de Santiago, 35A, 24526 Las
Herrerías, León, Spain

+34 987 13 49 15

Amenities: Private bedroom with bathroom,
bathtub upon request, lounge area with fireplace, restaurant serving dinner and breakfast

Daily thought: *Smile.*

I am noticing that the simple act of smiling holds incredible power, fostering a meaningful connection between
strangers. And as I near Santiago, I am also noticing
increased activity in places like cafés due to the influx of
more Pilgrims. Today's adventure led me to a seemingly
packed café with no available seats—that is until I shared
a smile with two fellow Pilgrims. Without my uttering a
single word to them, I was offered an invitation—"Would
you like to sit with us?"—reminding me of the pro-
found impact a genuine smile can have in creating a sense
of camaraderie.

Camino Message

*"It does not matter how slow you go,
so long as you do not stop."*
—CONFUCIUS

DAY 31:

Las Herrerías to O Cebreiro—9 km/5.6 mi

La Venta Celta
Rúa Cebreiro, 27670, O Cebreiro, Spain
+34 671 78 81 48
Amenities: Private bedroom with bathroom, TV, bar and garden, restaurant serving meals and continental breakfast

Daily thought: *Walk at your own pace.*

I woke up with a sense of nervous anticipation this morning, as today's journey was to be marked by the challenging mountain climb to O Cebreiro. But I reminded myself that I'd already secured lodging at the mountain's summit and had only a manageable 5.6 miles ahead of me—so, instead of rushing out the door with my fellow Pilgrims, I indulged in a leisurely breakfast, followed by a calming meditation and stretching session, before embarking on the day's delightful hike. I went at my own pace toward the peak of O Cebreiro, resisting the urge to speed up; I've learned that taking breaks and staying hydrated are key to avoiding burnout on walking days. Plus, going more slowly allowed me to enjoy the beauty of my incredible climb through the clouds at the top of the mountain.

Camino Message

"You keep putting one foot in front of another, and then one day you look back and you have climbed a mountain."
—Tom Hiddleston

DAY 32:

O Cebreiro to Triacastela—21 km/13.04 mi

Casa David

Avenida Camilo Jose Cela 8, 27630 Triacastela,
Spain

+34 982 54 81 44

$54

Amenities: Private bedroom with bathroom,
TV, bathtub upon request, bar, snack bar,
washer and dryer, breakfast

Daily thought: *Getting to town early? Make a plan.*
Descending the mountain today, I reached the charming
town of Triacastela. At the town's entrance, I encountered
my three preferred services: a massage clinic, a restaurant,
and a laundromat. If there's one piece of advice I can
share with you, dear reader, it's to swiftly book reservations at the clinic (you'll find their number on the front
door) and at the restaurant just across the street upon
arriving in town. And you might as well drop off your
dirty clothes at the laundromat too. By midday today,
both the clinic and the restaurant were fully booked, and
a line had formed at the laundromat (which, I'm told, is
business as usual). Planning ahead saved me from missing
out on all three—and trust me, these services are all very
much needed at the end of the day!

Camino Message

*"Sometimes you find yourself in the
middle of nowhere, and sometimes in the
middle of nowhere you find yourself."*
—ANONYMOUS

DAY 33:

Triacastela to Sarria—19 km/11.4 mi via San Xil or 25 km/15.52 mi via Samos

Hotel Alfonso IX

Rúa do Peregrino, 29, 27600 Sarria, Spain

+34 982 53 00 05

$81

Amenities: Private bedroom with bathroom, air-conditioning, TV, fitness center and pool, twenty-four-hour front desk, restaurant serving traditional Galician cuisine and breakfast

Daily thought: *Enjoy yourself!*

Today marks my final day of walking with fewer people, as most Pilgrims commence their Camino pilgrimage in Sarria. I've decided to savor every moment, taking my time to appreciate the beauty of the woods, the serenity of the farms, and the presence of the farm animals. While I anticipate that my walking experience will undergo a transformation and require adjustments in the days to come, I'm resolutely focused on enjoying what's before me today—relishing every experience and the unique delights they bring.

Camino Message

"A mind that is stretched by a new experience can never go back to its old dimensions."
—Oliver Wendell Holmes

DAY 34:
Sarria to Portomarín—22.3 km/13.8 mi

Hotel Ferramenteiro

Av. Chantada, 3, 27170 Portomarín, Spain

+34 982 54 53 61

$97

Amenities: Private bedroom with bathroom, TV, air-conditioning, bathtub upon request, bar, terrace, laundry, buffet breakfast

Daily thought: *Hello, new Pilgrims. It's nice to meet you.* As I enter the home stretch of my journey, the number of Pilgrims on the Camino (including my husband) has increased and the dynamic of the Camino has shifted significantly, just as I anticipated. To navigate this change, I have adopted a few new strategies:

Bring more snacks: Considering the increased number of people everywhere I go, carrying food for snacks and picnics outside is proving to be a great way to enjoy meals without the rush of busy restaurants.

Step aside for large groups: If large walking groups encroach on my personal space, I simply step aside and let them pass.

Share a smile and *"Buen Camino"*: Together, a warm smile and this familiar greeting create a sense of camaraderie with new Pilgrims, fostering a positive atmosphere on the journey.

Embrace a positive perspective: I keep reminding myself that a world with more Pilgrims is a better world. Each new face adds to the collective experience. The world would be a better place if everyone were a Pilgrim.

By incorporating these approaches, I find I can navigate this new version of the journey with grace and continue to appreciate the unique essence of the Camino, even in its final stages.

> **Camino Message**
> *"Somewhere between the start
> of the trail and the end is the mystery
> of why we choose to walk."*
> —Anonymous

DAY 35:

Portomarín to Palas de Rei—25 km/15.4 mi

Casa Leopoldo
Calle de la Paz 2, 27200 Palas de Rei, Lugo, Spain
+34 671 96 26 66
$158 (Booked directly at www.casaleopoldo-caminodesantiago.com)
Amenities: Private bedroom with bathroom, TV, lounge area, breakfast

Daily thought: *Casa Leopoldo and Pasta Restaurant are THE BEST.*

Today, I have a special recommendation for fellow Pilgrims: consider staying at Casa Leopoldo and dining at Pasta Restaurant. I can personally vouch for Cas Leopoldo's exceptionally comfortable beds and delightful fine-dining breakfast experience. I won't spoil the surprise by revealing the menu; just trust me, it's fantastic.

For dinner, I highly recommend checking out Pasta Restaurant. My husband and I had the pleasure of dining there during its opening week. From the enthusiastic owner to the enjoyable atmosphere and the flavorful pasta dishes, it was one of my favorite meal experiences on the Camino. If you find it open, there's no need to research other dining options; simply go—and let them know California Andrea sent you!

Camino Message

"Explore the world with an open mind, a sturdy carry-on, and clothes that don't wrinkle."
—Madeleine Albright

DAY 36:

Palas de Rei to Arzúa—28.5 km/17.7 mi

Hotel Suiza

Rúa Rio Vello, s/n, Arzúa, Spain

+34 981 50 09 08

$67

Amenities: Private bedroom with bathroom, TV, restaurant, bar, garden terrace

Daily thought: *Sometimes, good enough is good enough.* Today proved to be a lengthy hike, exacerbated by the fact that my hotel is situated on the outside of town. The silver lining, however, is that tomorrow's trek will be shorter, and we will most likely be ahead of some of the crowds.

As for Hotel Suiza, it's a bit of a mixed bag. Is it glamorous? No. Is it clean? Yes. Does it have a restaurant? Yes. We skipped dinner but are planning on enjoying coffee and croissants before heading out for the day, and I'm glad we don't have to go looking for somewhere to do that.

The moral of the story? This might not be your most luxurious stay, but it served its purpose. I had an excellent night's sleep, and sometimes that's all you really need on the Camino.

> **Camino Message**
> *"The end of a journey means
> the start of another one."*
> —THE BOOK OF FELICITY

DAY 37:
Arzúa to Rúa/O Pedrouzo—19.3 km /12 mi

Albergue Mirador de Pedrouzo

Avenida de Lugo s/n, 15821 O Pedrouzo, Spain

+34 686 87 12 15

$76

Amenities: Bunk bedrooms (you can rent the entire room if so desired), shared bathroom, air-conditioning, bar, shared lounge, garden, pool, and washer and dryer

Daily thought: *If you don't love the place you've booked, explore other places to stay.*

To be fair, Albergue Mirador de Pedrouzo is an okay place—it just didn't quite meet my preferences. It's a hostel with only bunk beds in its rooms. As a small person, I didn't mind the bunk beds, but my husband's longer legs extended well beyond the foot of the bed. Thankfully, we were able to rent a room to ourselves. The shared bathroom was another aspect that didn't quite live up to expectations, as fellow Pilgrims left it in a messy state and the shower wasn't draining well, resulting in a flooded floor.

The most significant disappointment for me, however, was the closed-off pool. I can't express how excited I was upon arrival, envisioning a refreshing swim in this magnificent pool, only to be halted by the sight of a sign that simply read, "Pool closed." So perhaps my opinion might have been different if it were open. I love a pool, especially after a long, hot day of walking.

The room itself was clean and the staff were friendly, making it sufficient for a one-night stay. Given the option, though, I would have opted for a different place.

> ## Camino Message
> *"Sometimes the longest journey we make is the 16 inches from our head to our heart."*
> —ELENA AVILA

DAY 38:
Rúa/O Pedrouzo to Santiago—19.4 km/12.1 mi

Hotel Montes

Rúa da Raiña, 11, 15704 Santiago de
Compostela, Spain

+34 981 57 44 58

$151

Amenities: Private bedroom with bathroom
and lounge area, TV, air-conditioning, bar, and
restaurant

Daily thoughts: *Do not rush. This is the moment. Take your time.*

On this final day, a myriad of emotions accompanies me. Despite the natural urge to hasten toward Santiago, to obtain my Compostela, and to revel in the celebration of having completed my quest, I am choosing the opposite: I am deliberately slowing down, allowing myself to absorb every nuance of this last day's journey. I know that with two days ahead of us in Santiago, I can afford to delay collecting my Compostela until tomorrow when the office opens at 9:00 a.m., especially since I have already preregistered online. I also know "this is it" as far as my Camino experience goes.

This is my opportunity to be truly present. To savor each step and to embrace the culmination of this remarkable Pilgrimage . . . when the time comes.

Camino Message
"The journey is the reward."
—Tao expression

Epilogue →

I've been home for nearly two months now, and my thoughts continue to gravitate back to my days on the Camino. I've found solace in sharing my experiences with strangers, recognizing that my friends may have grown weary of hearing me start yet another sentence with, "So when I was on the Camino . . ." My Camino obsession has even led me to follow and participate in more Camino Facebook group discussions, offering insights and answers—and absorbing those of other Pilgrims—to keep that connection alive.

There's a part of me that wants to prolong this adventure indefinitely, is tempted even to conjure up new stories just to sustain the feeling of being on the Camino, that truly magical place. However, the time has come for me to bring this chapter of my journey to a close and hand over the metaphorical reins to you.

Reflecting on my journey, I ponder whether there's anything I would have done differently on the Camino. The answer is yes. While I absolutely loved my Camino experience, the essence of any endeavor undertaken lies in the lessons learned. So what *were* some of those lessons, you might wonder?

I'm so glad you asked:

1. **Ask more questions:** I'd be more proactive inquiring about things like whether breakfast was included at my accommodations and if I could arrange a packed lunch for the next day.

2. **Research dining options:** I'd dedicate time to researching places to eat and purchase food, aiming for a more diverse and nutritious selection, including a variety of fruits and vegetables.

3. **Schedule rest days:** I'd schedule rest days in places I'd like to explore further, allowing for a deeper and more enriching experience.

4. **Plan with fellow Pilgrims:** I'd make a conscious effort to plan more meals and walks with fellow Pilgrims, fostering deeper connections and shared moments along the journey.

5. **Do more homework on my destinations:** I'd conduct a bit more research on the "must-see things" in each village—including asking fellow Pilgrims for their recommendations—to ensure I didn't miss out on any hidden gems or cultural landmarks.

6. **Learn the language:** Recognizing the value of communication, I'd invest time in at least learning more Spanish than I had mastered when I went, to facilitate interactions with both locals and Spanish-speaking Pilgrims.

7. **Express gratitude:** At the end of each day, I'd make it a habit to look up at the sky and

express gratitude, acknowledging the beauty of the journey and the lessons it brings.

8. **Stay longer:** I know not everyone can take long chunks of time off, and thirty-eight days is nothing to sniff at—I just wish I'd had a bit longer.

9. **Do it:** For the longest time, I said to myself, "I will walk the Camino when the time is right," and had every excuse in the book about how to put it off even longer—I let fear hold me back. Don't be like me; don't put your life on hold. Just do it. The Camino is a gift that will keep giving long after you leave the trail.

10. **Plan the next one!**

Walking the Camino transformed my body, mind, and soul. It's your turn now.

It's my great honor to be the first to say, "*Buen Camino.*"

Inspiration Letter →

This letter was written by my friend and fellow Pilgrim Charina (a.k.a. one of the two Marias) whom I met while walking and now hold as a lifelong friend. I hope you find it as inspiring as I do!

Dear Pilgrim,

Even if you have not taken that first step to walk the Camino yet, the fact that you are reading this means you have already taken that first step. You are already a Pilgrim.

It took me more than a decade to finally walk the Camino Frances. The Camino first came into my consciousness in my late thirties, but at that time, I told myself that I was not ready. I had two young boys, the eldest of whom had an intellectual disability. I had a full-time career. My hands were full. I felt tethered, undeserving of a break, trapped in my family life, unable to make a decision that felt selfish at that time. A decade passed—and a pandemic happened. So many people I knew passed away. I felt the familiar Camino tug at my heart. But this time, the calling was louder, more persistent. I felt as if I were running out of time.

And now, the kids are in their early twenties and my career is in a steady state. I had run out of excuses not to walk the Camino.

In order to complete the full 800-kilometer distance of the Camino, they say you must have a strong *why*. Walking what usually turns out to be at least 20 kilometers a day is a physical grind. There is cumulative fatigue. And I had other doubts too: Was it safe for a woman to walk alone? I had never been to Spain, and I didn't speak the language—where would I sleep? What would happen if I got injured? Would I get lost? Were there signs along the way, and were they easy to follow? Did I really have to carry my own pack?

These questions held me captive!

People walk the Camino for various reasons. Some walk it to make a change in their lives, whether it's a change of pace, scenery, relationships, or life trajectory. Others walk it to find a sense of purpose and meaning, to journey toward wholeness and self-expression. The Camino provides a unique perspective on life, helping walkers see what truly matters and what doesn't.

Personally, I wanted to walk the Camino to reconnect with my true nature. I wanted to walk out of my life and the different roles I play as a mother, caregiver, wife, daughter, friend, worker. I wanted to be the old me—little, twelve-year-old Richie.

Ultimately, my *why* far outweighed all my fears of the unknown.

If there are any obstacles holding *you* back, I hope this guidebook will shatter them. Because walking the Camino was a transformative experience. Every day, I met, walked, and dined with people whom I bonded with over our shared experience. When you are on the Camino, you become open to whatever the day brings. The only requirement each day is to walk, eat, and sleep. It's freeing.

As you walk, you will learn to trust people you have never met before. One day, I walked with an Italian woman who did not speak English, yet we connected with and supported each other. It was magical. I also felt held and supported by the local community as I walked from village to village. The Camino will bring back your faith in humanity. It will also give you the time and space to explore your inner landscape.

I won't lie to you—it will not be perfect. You will encounter problems along the Way. But isn't that what makes life interesting?

Stay curious; don't be afraid of the unknown. Prepare yourself by training your body and your mind. Take the leap.

Go ahead and make the decision to walk the Camino, dear Pilgrim—and then trust that decision, and hold fast to it.

Buen Camino!

Love,
Charina

Resources →

In addition to this book, numerous excellent resources, ranging from apps to websites, are available to assist you in planning your Camino journey. Here are a handful of them that I found useful!

Apps I Recommend ➔

Books: Audible

Communication: WhatsApp

Maps: Buen Camino de Santiagoa

Maps: Camino Ninja

Mobile Guidebook: Wise Pilgrim All Caminos

Meditation: Insight Timer

Weather: iPhone Weather, AccuWeather

Websites I Recommend →

Accommodation directory including available amenities: www.caminosleeps.com

General information/Pilgrim Passport/Compostela registration: www.caminodesantiago.me

General information: www.americanpilgrims.org

Guidebook: https://viajecaminodesantiago.com/en

Luggage transport and taxi service: www.caminofacil.net

Sleep accommodation: www.booking.com

Women's buddy system Camigas: www.facebook.com/groups/CaminoBuddySystemForWomen

Women over 50 support group: www.facebook.com/groups/woacathecamino

About the Author

Andrea Wait has traveled to the Camino de Santiago on four different occasions, exploring the Portuguese Way, the French Way, and most recently, the full 500-mile journey over forty-three days. She's navigated blisters and self-doubt, missed reservations, and experienced the transformative kindness of strangers. Throughout her Camino travels, she has shared parts of the trail with friends—both old and new—and her husband, John, but she has always planned her trips solo and spent many days walking alone. This book is a culmination of the questions she's been asked as a solo woman traveling the Camino—how she prepared for it, how she planned it, how she felt being alone, and how she handled, and learned to embrace, the unexpected.

Andrea's goal in writing this book is to empower women considering a walk on the Camino. Having been drawn to the Camino de Santiago for many years, she considers it to be one of the most transformative journeys of her life, and she hopes to help other women interested in walking believe that they can do it too.

When she's not writing or planning adventures, Andrea can be found walking with her husband around the neighborhoods of San Francisco or exploring some of the many other wonders of Northern California.

Andrea Wait is also the author of *Home in Harmony: A Practical Guide to Organizing*.

Author photo: Courtesy of the author